THE Revd Dr Mark Clavier, who has dual British–US citizenship, is Dean of Residential Training at St Michael's College, Llandaff. Before moving to the UK in 2008, Dr Clavier served in parishes in Maryland and North Carolina. Since then, he has served as a house-for-duty priest in County Durham and as priest-in-charge of three churches in Oxford diocese.

RESCUING THE CHURCH FROM CONSUMERISM

MARK CLAVIER

First published in Great Britain in 2013

Society for Promoting Christian Knowledge
36 Causton Street
London SW1P 4ST
www.spckpublishing.co.uk

British Library Cataloguing-in-Publication Data
A catalogue record for this book is available from the British Library

ISBN 978–0–281–07038–1
eBook ISBN 978–0–281–07039–8

Typeset by Graphicraft Limited, Hong Kong

eBook by Graphicraft Limited, Hong Kong

Produced on paper from sustainable forests

Contents

Preface

One of my favourite saints is St Columbanus, the Irish monk who 'peregrinated' to continental Europe at the end of the sixth century. By all accounts, he was a prickly customer with little patience for the customs he encountered among Gallic Christians. Coming as he did from Ireland, he represented a 'backwater' Christianity that few in Continental Europe would have taken seriously. Ireland itself was off the map for most people in Europe – they generally thought of the Irish as vulgar and barbaric – and so Columbanus must have appeared as a kind of curiosity when he first presented himself to the Burgundian court. What must he have made of the church in Gaul with its massive basilica churches and masses of donated wealth? The Irish church had nothing much to compare with the wealth of the mainstream Catholic Church. What Columbanus's church did have, however, was optimism and confidence, a zeal for the gospel, a devotion to learning, and success at rapidly transforming a venerable pagan society. By contrast, the much larger and mainstream church he encountered in Burgundy was in cultural decline, still reeling from the collapse of empire and barbarian invasions, unsure of itself or of its role in a newly de-urbanized society.

While I am certainly no saint, I feel some sympathy for St Columbanus. Like him, I 'peregrinated' from the frontier to a long-established church – only with me, I came from the 'backwaters' of Continuing Anglicanism to the Established Church of England. Prior to my arrival in the UK in 2008, I had been a priest in a tiny, conservative Anglican jurisdiction that seeks to preserve traditional Anglicanism and the Book of Common Prayer. In fact, I was the first priest to have been raised entirely within one of the so-called Continuing Anglican churches. This, and the fact that my father was a bishop in one of these jurisdictions, meant that I had grown into adulthood surrounded by the controversies that have beset The Episcopal Church, worshipping for most of that time in living rooms, shop fronts and newly constructed church buildings, with the American 1928 Book of Common Prayer and the 1940 Hymnal as the twin pillars of my devotional life. Thus, the Anglican identity that is bound up in glorious buildings, sweet-sounding choirs, lavish vesture and an easy relationship with the Establishment was as foreign to me as the Gallic church must have been to Columbanus and his Irish companions. The Anglicanism I knew before moving to the UK was one stripped down to its basics: crudely built or reused altars, old prayer books with broken spines, crudely woven vestments and altar hangings, and clergy who worked in second jobs in order to earn a living wage. It was also isolated from much of the rest of the Christian world: the liturgical movement, 30 years of hymnody, popular theologians and authors, and countless devotional fashions passed me by entirely. I was 37 years old before I began regularly to worship with a liturgy in which the response to 'The Lord be with you' was not 'And with thy spirit'. I was slightly older before I attended my first continuing education day for clergy, had to cope with diocesan bureaucracies, or regularly encountered Anglicans whose theology was shaped by contemporary people and movements. Finally, I had cut my theological eye teeth entirely on 'out-of-date' Anglicans: C. S. Lewis was followed by T. S. Eliot and Dorothy Sayers before I dived more deeply into Richard Hooker, Lancelot Andrewes, the Caroline divines, Jeremy Taylor, George Herbert, Charles Gore, William Temple and Michael Ramsey. Thus, my conception and articulation of Anglicanism was in a shape and form that no longer really existed. At the advanced age of 37, I came to the UK as both a liturgical and a theological anachronism. When I walked into our local parish church on the first Sunday after our arrival, I was not unlike Rip Van Winkle after his 20-year nap.

While the battles and objectives of the Continuing Anglican movement are no longer my own, the fellowship and optimism that I experienced in their churches, both as a child and as a parish priest for 12 years, left a deep imprint on me. I didn't realize just how profound this was until I returned to the active ministry in the Church of England. I found myself unsuspectingly voicing questions that few seemed to ask any more. Where are the children serving at the altar? How are we organizing our pancake supper? Is there an altar guild? How are teenagers taught the catechism? The liturgical culture in which I was formed was almost entirely gone and in many cases forgotten. Echoes and shadows of a more familiar Anglicanism surrounded me – old, child-sized albs, disused devotionals and discarded ornate vestments – but few seemed to notice them. I would pick hymns set to English tunes and composed by English men and women for services that remain familiar in many churches in the USA only to discover that here in the UK hardly anyone under the age of 45 knew them. In fact, elderly parishioners were typically the people with whom I most identified; for their part, they seemed to enjoy my old-fashioned ways and received me as one welcomes home an old friend.

I suppose the cantankerous St Columbanus would not have approved of all these changes. For my part, when I moved to the UK, I was determined to be open-minded about them; indeed, some I welcomed immediately, particularly the less stodgy inclusion of the laity in worship (in my former existence, laity still had to wear cassock and surplice even to read a lesson). I adapted quickly to changes great and small: women clergy, a new liturgy, facing the people over the altar when celebrating, hymns dating from a supposed golden era of the 1960s and 1970s, charging fees for sacramental rites, and much less operative discretion at the parish level. Now, that list alone will cause some to dismiss me as a bit of a fuddy-duddy (which I suppose I am). My only response is that even had I embraced all these changes enthusiastically, I still would have had to adapt. As St Columbanus didn't choose to be born in Ireland and formed in the Irish church, so too did I not choose to be born in the USA and formed within a traditional Anglican jurisdiction.

Those were innovations that I was in some ways prepared to meet when I came to the UK. I was much less prepared for the narrative of decline and lack of ecclesial self-confidence that I encountered in some quarters of the Church of England. I had come from a tiny jurisdiction confident in its message, active and engaging in its ministry, and certain of its future. We took it as read that our congregations would increase in size, that we would eventually raise the funds to pay clergy full-time stipends and build lovely churches, and that even in a modern age young people could be drawn to an old Prayer Book and ceremonial worship. Considering our limited resources, the inherent unwillingness of conservatives to take risks, and the complete disregard for inculturation demonstrated by an insistence on an old Prayer Book and antiquated ceremonial, it was astonishing that we could be so confident. Though I have no regrets about coming to the UK, I miss that boundless optimism, love of Anglicanism and sheer pleasure of caring for souls, especially because more often than not we were right: our churches did grow and, in many cases, became anchored in deeply committed groups of young families.

In contrast, the Church I encountered here in the UK, far richer, larger and omnipresent than anything I'd ever experienced before, seemed demoralized, in some places even despairing of its future, with little sense of itself or of its role in the world. That may be an unfair assessment, but it was what struck me most powerfully coming from my peculiar background. When asked during a conference to compare parish ministry here to that in the USA, I replied, 'It feels like I've gone from herding springer spaniels to herding basset hounds!' Inertia has taken hold of a great deal of British Anglicanism, due partly, I believe, to that now long narrative of decline and partly to the morass of bureaucratic rules and regulations that bog down initiatives. That inertia stands out all the more starkly because I have found that the people in the pews here are much like those I cared for in the USA and have responded to my antiquated approach to ministry in exactly the same way. That, at least, does not surprise me because I believe that underneath various cultural accretions people remain much the same. One of the greatest delusions of any culture or generation is that its members are somehow different from all others. That delusion, I believe, is too often accepted by those who advocate adjusting to cultural expectations in order to remain relevant. As they say in the American South, 'People is people.' Ministry in suburban Maryland, semi-rural North Carolina, post-industrial County Durham and rural Oxfordshire has shown me how true that is.

My unusual Anglican background and my experience as an outsider in the Church of England provide part of the context for this study. Much that I have included in the second part of this book comes from my observations and experiences in the Church of England as an outsider and remnant of an older form of Anglicanism; I am, if you will, a rather young Ghost of Christmas Past. The first part of this book grew out of an equally profound journey that began a few years after the birth of my son, soon after my arrival in the beautiful mountains of western North Carolina. In October 2002, I decided that it was time to pull myself away from the computer and go for a walk in the Pisgah National Forest. Like so many Americans, I had grown overly attached to the sofa, had gained a fair amount of weight and found myself (despite the many blessings of my life) feeling empty and alone. I'm not sure what drew me to go hiking that day, but the experience of being alone in the forested Blue Ridge Mountains awoke something deep within me that has never gone back to sleep. I discovered delight, that overpowering and uncontrollable enjoyment of something for its own sake. That tiring but exhilarating day's walk (followed by many more) taught me that my emptiness wasn't something just psychological or accidental, but was the direct result of a life too consumed by the need to be entertained and stimulated. Walking alone for hours surrounded by the beauty of nature does something wonderful for the mind and soul – or at least it does for mine. It reconnected me with the world – that natural creation that underpins all our human constructions but that we so easily neglect – and subsequently both with God and myself. That one walk to Ivestor Gap on a frosty autumn day completely changed my life.

Afterwards, while providing spiritual direction for young adults, I realized that I had not been alone in my feelings of emptiness and isolation. I repeatedly encountered people whose lives were dominated by television, console games, the Internet and stimulating music, and who felt the same emptiness that I had felt. Like me, they had become largely inured to delight, which, like prayer, they found too slow and boring to appreciate. Through these conversations, I became convinced that there is a correlation between the volume of entertainment in our lives and the distance that God seems to stand apart from us. Perhaps God's still, small voice is too soft to be heard beneath the cacophony of our media-saturated lives.

That insight came to me as I re-emerged into the normal world following a short retreat at Mepkin Abbey, the Trappist monastery in Monck's Corner, South Carolina, in 2007. After several days of quiet contemplation, prayer, walks in the gardens and daily rounds of monastic offices, I was struck powerfully by the ugliness of modern life. Why is it that so much of it clashes with our natural world? Cheaply constructed buildings, shopping centres, criss-crossing telephone and electric cables, speeding cars, blaring radios, garish hoardings and cast-off rubbish all assaulted my senses as I drove back home. It brought to mind that part of *The Lord of the Rings* when the Hobbits return to the Shire only to find that it has been turned into an industrial slum by Saruman. Thanks to my short time in the company of monks, I was able for the briefest of moments to glimpse our consumer culture as an outsider might. So, I decided I would begin seriously to consider the question of delight. To my surprise, this led me quickly to the medieval mystics, especially Aelred of Rievaulx, Bonaventure and Julian of Norwich. Unlike modern theology, their works are filled with delight; the idea appears repeatedly in their writings to describe God, creation and our relationship with one another. Say what you will about some of their notions about sin and judgement, their overarching vision of redeemed humanity living in joyful harmony with God and creation is very attractive. Their whole conception of reality was based not on power struggles or exploitation but on a love that both fills and transcends all creation. Their writings opened up to me a whole new world that resonated with my personal experience of delight and that subsequently deepened my concern about both the dehumanizing effects of consumer culture and the Church's failure to challenge it.

This discovery of delight led directly to my departure from Continuing Anglicanism and my move to the UK to pursue a doctorate. Winston Churchill once said that in heaven he wanted to get to the bottom of colour; I wanted to get to the bottom of delight. Thus, I arrived with my family in wonderful Durham to spend nearly three years theologically examining delight. It still astonishes me that my wife, Diane, was willing to go along with this! Day after day, I immersed myself in the writings of Augustine, Anselm, Richard of St Victor, Bonaventure and Julian of Norwich, growing more and more familiar with their vision of a divine delight that underpins all creation. Their notion of a world suffused with God's own delight and of a deity who is supreme Delight opened my eyes to a vision of a church capable of offering an alternative to our relentless need to consume in order to have an identity. I did not realize it at the time, but this vision had also reordered my priorities. I found that I no longer felt strongly about the various debates that perpetually afflict Anglicanism and that had dominated so much of my life. Rightly or wrongly, I came to see these debates not as a solution to our problems but as a symptom – we find them impossible to resolve because a great deal of our desires, convictions, assumptions and rhetoric have been deeply affected by our shared consumer culture.

The impetus to turn my experience and reflections into a book arose from a paper on liturgical consumerism I gave at the 2009 Michael Vasey Conference at St John's College, Durham. The conference provided me with the opportunity to think about the approach to worship I had often encountered since coming to the UK. Much of it was very foreign to me. After all, up to 2008, I had lived my entire life within a church community sheltered from 70 or more years of liturgical renewal. One thing we never asked was how our services might attract people or be made more accessible. We won people to our churches – and, as traditional Anglicans we had to work hard just to get people to walk through our church doors – through our warm fellowship and hospitality. Only later did many of these people come to love our liturgy as its words and symbols wove themselves into their hearts and minds. Despite my acceptance of the broader liturgical worship of the Church of England, I felt instinctively that this notion was basically right. One of the cornerstones of Anglicanism is the idea that the liturgy – 'common prayer' – is one of the primary sources of unity and identity within the Church. That does not mean that we must continue to use the Book of Common Prayer, but it does suggest that our liturgical expression should be much more than a means of self-promotion, advertisement or corporate sentiment.

Just as importantly, in the course of researching that paper, I discovered many of the sociological analyses that underpin the arguments of the first section of this book. The insights that I read in these books and articles have been largely untapped in theological discussions about society, especially when compared with the monumental influence of modern philosophy and the life sciences on our theological discussions. In particular, Vincent Miller's *Consuming Religion* enabled me to ponder the Church's role within consumer culture and the ways that it has allowed itself to become absorbed into that culture. I also became increasingly dissatisfied with the notions of 'postmodernism' and 'postmodernity' that fill the pages of contemporary theology; it seems to me that, more often than not, postmodernism is really just consumerism dressed up in posh, philosophical clothes. That is why the term appears almost nowhere in this book. Most importantly, reading sociological discussions of consumerism caused me to begin considering whether consumer culture is best understood as a religion – a highly destructive one, too – that needs to be better understood and challenged.

And so, the experience of an optimistic, familial church (however misguided one may consider its efforts), my theological exploration of delight and my growing belief that consumer culture makes the same claims on identity as any religion have come together to produce this book. There is probably much idealism to be found in the following pages, but also (I hope) much realism grounded in a parish ministry spanning the better part of two decades. There is nothing in this book that is not based to some extent on my own experience of parochial ministry in various communities in two different countries. Moreover, as I have discussed my thoughts with others during the past six or seven years, I have found that they resonate with many, which is what has led me to cast aside my usual diplomacy and to make my case as clearly and convincingly as I can. Nearly five years of parish ministry in the UK, first in former pit villages of County Durham and then among the charming honey-toned villages of rural Oxfordshire, has only strengthened my conviction that we desperately need to find our old confidence and sense of mission to redeem the lives of people caught up in the destructive impulses of fallen humanity. Until we begin to offer the lost souls of our consumer culture that abundant delight that is woven into the fabric of creation and is none other than the glory of God himself, I suspect we'll continue to be the self-obsessed and self-doubting church we are often perceived to be.

As this short autobiography may indicate, there are many people that I should acknowledge for this book. I will begin with John Pritchard, the Bishop of Oxford, who showed interest in my manuscript and suggested I submit it to SPCK. Likewise, I am grateful to Alison Barr, my editor, whose patient advice has improved the book immeasurably. Next, I owe an enormous debt to my theological companions of many years: Erich Zwingert, Mike Ward, Glenn Spencer, Dan Martins, Christopher Wells, Craig Uffman, Jeremy Bergstrom and, above all others, Paul Blankenship. Long discussions with Mike and Paul over the formative years of my musings did much to shape my later ideas. In that respect, like so many others, I also owe a huge debt to Tom Wright and Rowan Williams, both of whose writings compelled me to emerge from my traditional Anglican cave and join the present-day theological conversation of the Church. I believe that the profound impact of Rowan Williams on Anglican theology has yet fully to be appreciated. Finally, I must acknowledge my family: my father, whose remarkable sermons probably influenced my theology more than anything else; my mother, whose quiet devotion to church and family inspired me; my wife Diane, who has patiently listened to me pontificate on consumerism over the years and has also supported me throughout that strange adventure that led us from the USA to England and now to Wales; and finally my son Paul, who has patiently endured my many lectures to him about spending too much time at the computer!

I am incredibly grateful to all my parishioners both past and present who have graciously accepted my ministry, forgiven my failings, shown my family and me tremendous love and affection, and who have taught me so much about the wonderful complexity of human nature. This book is dedicated to them in gratitude for the fellowship I have been privileged to share with them – more than anything else, that fellowship has taught me what it means to be part of the household of God.

1

The cult of consumerism

The world has rarely if ever witnessed a country with the missionary zeal of the USA. Evangelists from an array of denominations have taken the good news to every continent in the world. Thanks in part to their efforts, countless souls have undoubtedly been won for Christ, and Christianity has become predominantly non-European for the first time since the rise of Islam during the seventh century. Americans have been just as eager to preach the civic gospel of 'truth, justice and the American Way'. The American ideals of individualism, democracy and the free market have been embraced the world over. US foreign policy, even at its most pragmatic, is typically draped in the banner of 'freedom and justice for all'. And, though there are many countries still recovering from US interventionism, many more now prosper either directly through US aid or indirectly by the power of the American ideal. The USA itself is peopled with the 'tired', 'poor' and 'huddled masses' of every nation drawn there by the 'American dream'. Yet, there is a third American movement that has reached deeply into the private lives of billions of people around the world and reshaped entire societies and cultures. The message of this movement is broadcast across television, radios, the Internet and in the airbrushed pages of magazines, is expressed in fashion, music, drama and many other ways, and shapes lives in a far more intimate and enduring way than any religion has ever done. It is, in fact, the single most powerful and pervasive religion the world has ever known: consumerism.

Most people do not think of consumerism in religious terms.[1] Yet, like any religion, consumerism shapes individual and collective lives, preaches an all-encompassing world-view, has its own rituals, and offers happiness as an ultimate reward for the initiated. That it is a religion broad enough to embrace both theists and atheists speaks to its incredible power to adapt and encompass almost any view,

1

philosophy or way of life. To live in a consumer society is to see the world as a consumer, think of oneself and others as consumers, and to seek happiness and fulfilment as a consumer. There is hardly anyone in the Western world who does not subscribe to consumerism. Even Marxists are happy to promote their products and market their ideals.

Consumerism, many will say, is a morally neutral phenomenon or, in fact, a manifest good because it promotes free enterprise and individual choice and spurs innovation. As evidence, one might offer the manifold luxuries that have become available to people from all walks of life during the past 50 years. Indeed, the technological creativity of the past 50 years has been spectacularly beyond anything the world has ever known. Would we have efficient automobiles, dishwashers, refrigerators, mobiles, flat-screen televisions, easily available foods, laptops and a universe of ingenious software, applications, console games and websites were it not for the energy fostered by a system that both creates and fulfils individual needs and desires and is driven by largely unregulated competition? Similarly, corporations and entrepreneurs have arguably achieved more for individual freedoms throughout the world than all the tanks, missiles and guns put together. Stalinism managed fairly well to stare down Western political pressure and military might but could do little against the invasion of Levi jeans and rock 'n' roll. An incredible amount of resources and single-minded devotion went into inculcating Marxist-Stalinist values into several generations of Russian and Eastern European children only to be swept away within a couple of decades as Eastern Europeans embraced the values of consumerism as eagerly as any American. Not even the Cultural Revolution of Mao Tse-tung could long withstand the lure of Western goods and services. One lesson the last 50 years has taught is that totalitarianism must either adapt or yield to consumer desires; it cannot long suppress them.

But granting the global achievements of consumerism does not necessarily contradict its inherently religious character. Historically, the only lasting movements that have resembled the rise and spread of consumerism have been religious ones. For example, the altar found at Broccolitia along Hadrian's Wall in northern England, carved with an image of the Persian god Mithras slaying a bull, is an evocative symbol of what might be called Roman religious consumerism. But it is the great monotheistic religions – especially Islam and

Christianity – that provide the nearest historical parallels to consumerism: both are international movements that either eclipse or transform local cultures. So, for example, Greeks who never entertained the idea of adopting 'barbaric' Jewish customs happily embraced the beliefs, practices and morals of Christianity and began to think of themselves as Christians. During the Middle Ages, a Europe that contained a chaotic mishmash of cultures shared a remarkably homogeneous religion that defined people both collectively and individually. Similarly, a quick flip through any hymn book will find a selection of music every bit as international as the selection of music on iTunes. Even as late as the twentieth century, soldiers from different countries determined to slaughter each other with technological savagery could celebrate together their shared Christian customs.

Consumerism has a similar capacity to introduce an alien culture into local communities in a way that transforms how the members of those communities understand themselves and their world. But consumerism is far more adaptable to different circumstances and cultures: once people begin to think of themselves as consumers, they are free to believe almost anything else they want. Consumerism can import almost any religion, ideology, culture or philosophy and transform it into mere lifestyle choices. All one has to do is look at the profits made in selling books about Marxism, or the marketing of anti-consumer periodicals, or the cost of books and seminars about living simply, to see that every attempt these days to promote a world-view other than consumerism just ends up being marketed and packaged into one among many lifestyles. No religion has ever had the capacity to adapt itself so readily to all its critics; no religion has ever so effectively impinged upon private lives, broadcast its core doctrines or turned its adherents into advocates.

One of the ways that religions transcend local culture is by connecting with people at the important moments and stages of their lives and situating those events in a larger narrative. Almost all religions have rites of passage and other rituals meant to provide meaning to important occasions or to imbue individual lives with higher meaning. Within Judaism, the Pesach, Shavuot and Sukkot place the lives of individuals and families within the Exodus narrative that establishes their collective identity as a covenanted people. Similarly, the Christian liturgical year seeks to ground people's lives in the Gospel narrative, and the sacramental system places meaningful occasions of social life within the context of God and the Church. The seven sacraments – baptism, confirmation, the Eucharist, marriage, ordination, reconciliation and holy unction – demarcate life's turning points and are believed to nourish the spirit.

In fact, the seven sacraments can function as a model of comparison to illustrate how consumerism shapes lives 'from cradle to grave' in the same way as religions. I will use them in the first part of this book to demonstrate in detail that consumerism is, indeed, a global religion. In order to map out a consumer's life according to a sacramental grid involves remarkably little translation. The reason for this speaks to the enduring character of the human condition and the ways in which we try to mark our life's journey: we are still born, grow into adulthood, enter into relationships, have children, and experience crises, suffering, old age and death. Thus, in order for consumerism to be widely embraced, it must, like any culture or religion, situate itself in the human condition. Equally, however, consumerism has transformed how we look at the pattern of everyday life just as much as any religion or culture. While Christianity has sought to recast childhood, adolescence, adult relationships, suffering and death within the overarching narrative of salvation and sanctification, consumerism seeks to recast them within the overarching narrative of desire, self-invention and identity; beginning in the cradle we imbibe the idea that we pursue happiness and identity through the purchase of products.

Sacraments are a foretaste of heaven and the means by which Christians undertake their journey towards salvation. Likewise, the 'sacraments' of consumerism are directed towards salvation, only now understood as the this-worldly promise of wellness, happiness and prosperity. The experience and promise of psychological, physical and financial happiness draw us more deeply into the cult of consumerism. That experience and promise also make it incredibly difficult for us to seek an alternative way of living. Among the most fervent Christians are those who have enjoyed a religious experience that has warmed their hearts. In that sense, members of the cult of consumerism have all had 'religious experiences' – such as the first drive in a new car, the playing of a new console game, a magical night out in a new dress – and continue to do so repeatedly.[2] Within religious communities, the testimony of people who have had religious experiences can be a powerful motivation for those stuck in spiritual doldrums. Similarly, one commercial after another portrays the sheer delight of purchase-moments, reminding us of similar experiences in our own lives and whetting our thirst for another. The ecstasies of these moments combine to make us keen consumers.

In the second part of this book, I will examine how Western Christianity, like every other aspect of Western culture, has been absorbed into consumerism and subsequently reshaped by and re-oriented towards expressing and promoting ideas, desires and hopes that have been drawn from consumer culture. Mainstream Christianity has often been reduced to a kind of spiritual expression of consumerism, at times deliberately in the hope that this will connect with the wider culture and breathe new life into a Church in decline. By both allowing itself to be reshaped by consumerism and failing to take a more critical stance against it, the Church has largely encouraged its own decline. Once Christianity allows itself to appear only as a lifestyle choice within the larger culture of consumerism, it surrenders its reason for existence and becomes merely a matter of consumer taste. Indeed, because the Christian gospel contains elements that are difficult to translate into consumerist values – not least its reliance on an ancient and non-upgradeable Scripture – churches almost inevitably end up being poor or amateurish expressions of consumerism. Why rely on churches to meet one's consumer needs when so many others do it with more facility?

In the final part of this book, I will argue that the Church needs to begin to conceive of itself apart from consumerism in order to fulfil its mission to the world. It will be my contention that at the local level and beneath fabricated 'expressions' of the Church can be found a deeper and more meaningful form of Christianity from which new life and vision can be nourished and enriched. Central to my argument is the idea of the *oikos*, or home, understood here as a visible, placed community with its own defining narrative, obligations and largely unchosen relationships. I will draw upon the theology of Stanley Hauerwas and the recent philosophical work of Roger Scruton to present a model of the Church that can free itself from consumer culture and begin to offer an alternative vision of society. The renewal of the Church must begin with a conversion of Christians away from consumerism so they can begin to perceive how compromised they are by a system that is inhumane and destructive both to society and the environment. That perception may then lead to a greater vision of faith that will satisfy the restless heart, draw people together into meaningful relationships and provide the foundation for a manner of living that is sustainable, transformative and revitalizing.

Consumer society

Perhaps the most striking and unusual characteristic of our world today is that instantaneous communication, swift and relatively inexpensive travel and easy access to information have created a global society that is intimately connected and intertwined. We speak now without irony of a global village. People are often more aware of the lives of others on an entirely different continent than of their own neighbours' lives. Music, literature, customs, ideas, films, diets, styles and fashions, and religious beliefs from an array of different cultures now intermingle in ways that influence not only one another but also individuals and local cultures. Indeed, the very idea of a 'remote' culture is increasingly meaningless as the Internet makes everyone more immediately present. Every culture impacted by television and the Internet is now a neighbour of each other, sharing its approach to life with cultures a world away just as much as geographical neighbours once did.

This would seem exciting, especially as historically the eras of cultural flourishing have almost always emerged from cross-cultural contacts. For example, the European Renaissance resulted partly from the fruitful contact between Christian and Muslim scholars during the high medieval period. Similarly, the scientific revolution of the eighteenth century depended largely on European expansion and exploration. Many critics, of course, point to the vapidity of much of our own cultural interaction. Certainly, it is deeply problematic to approach cultures as marketplaces where we can pick and choose various cultural artefacts, detached from their original setting, and employ them as we like. Nor is the sharing of culture anything like a meeting of equals; far more cultures are affected by American cosmopolitan culture than the reverse. In at least one way, however, globalization of culture is becoming less shallow. No longer is choosing another culture over one's own a deliberate (and often artificial) act made in adulthood (like middle-class Americans in the 1970s embracing Native American clothes and practices). Children today are growing up influenced by a number of different cultures almost from birth. The music a child listens to may have African, American, European and Asian elements to it, the clothes she wears may draw upon styles from a number of different places, and she may develop a distinctly international diet, as accustomed to Chinese, Indian and Italian food as she is to roast beef and Yorkshire pudding. A small child may read or listen to stories from the world over, later enjoy books translated from many different languages, and inhabit virtual worlds with people from almost every continent. And for an increasing number of these children, the Internet, with its doorway to worldwide cultures, products and individuals, provides the backdrop to everything they do. But this pluriform culture is not connected to any particular place; it exists largely in a consumer-created ecosystem detached from geography, locality and any fixed meaning. In so far as the individual will have experienced the cultural mixture in a unique way, that cultural milieu will also be deeply personalized. At a certain level, culture is now individualized; it is now my culture rather than our culture. Because a culture of one makes little sense, we now refer to this personalized and largely aesthetic culture as a 'lifestyle'.

The emergence of the concept of 'lifestyle', promoted in a popular sense during the 1960s and 1970s, is a key part of understanding consumerism as a religion. Although the various strands that led to the development of the concept of lifestyles are both complex and fascinating (and presented well in Adam Curtis's documentary *The Century of the Self*), there isn't space here to rehearse it in detail.[3] Its roots lie in the emergence of the field of public relations in the late 1940s, spearheaded by Edward Bernays, a nephew of Sigmund Freud, who saw that Freudian psychology could be used to shape public opinion and desires. He and others popularized the idea that the true force at work in society is not the rational discourse envisioned by America's Founding Fathers but subconscious forces often beyond individual control. Bernays's revolutionary idea was that, by appealing to and influencing the subconscious self, one can manage society and shape its expectations. He expressed this clearly in a short article written in 1938 on how free enterprise could be used to promote democracy:

> an automobile can be presented in terms of its larger significance to democracy – in terms of the greater freedom of motion it offers to individuals and groups, at a cost within the reach of

all income groups in the nation. Freedom of motion brings with it facilities for the freer exchange of ideas, a greater opportunity to see and experience how other groups in other localities live and meet their problems. This interchange of ideas and knowledge, brought about by more extensive, quicker, and cheaper transportation in any of its forms, thus ... becomes a conduit for democratic thought and ideas. The automobile can be shown, as well, in its relation to the democracy – its contribution to taxes and the use made of them for the people. The automobile thus becomes more than a mechanism on wheels – it becomes an instrument of democracy.[4]

It is not by accident that following the Second World War, the car and the open road became powerful symbols of freedom in the USA. Bernays and others went on to use their Freudian insights to transform advertising. This was the age that produced the first advertisements presenting their products as lifestyle symbols: the now familiar image of the happy and beautiful housewife using a branded vacuum cleaner surrounded by polite well-groomed children and a handsome husband, or the rugged-looking man driving a large 4×4 and smoking a cigarette. Advertisements such as these no longer simply displayed products for sale but presented, for subconscious consumption, an ideal world in which products were situated. People began to crave the portrayed idealized world and they subconsciously associated various products as necessary props of that world; buy the product, gain that happy world.[5]

During the 1950s and 1960s, however, humanistic or 'Third Force' psychologists like Abraham Maslow, Carl Rogers and Rollo May broke away from the established Freudian consensus that subconscious motivational forces needed to be controlled because of their often destructive nature.[6] This was the age of student movements and civil rights protests, in which the State and corporations were seen as at best problematic and at worst destructive to a truly flourishing society. The new humanistic psychologists proposed that people are inherently good and that psychic wholeness comes through the expression of the inner self. Increasingly, freedom and individual 'flourishing' were conceived in terms of removing the various barriers implanted by society – such as the State, family obligations and big business – that prevent individuals from 'self-actualization'. So, while the older guard of psychologists located evil within the individual, the new located it within society. Central to this new form of psychology was the idea that freedom – formerly defined in terms of political life – pertains to the individual's ability to choose whatever life he or she desires without undue constraints.

Thus, almost without knowing it, Western society experienced one of the profoundest cultural and intellectual revolutions since the emergence of Christianity. From at least the time of ancient Greece, the fundamental intellectual quest of individuals and societies was encapsulated by the Delphic command, 'Know thyself'. Wisdom, perceived as the highest virtue, was obtained through self-knowledge. The means of achieving that self-knowledge might differ but all agreed that people had an objective, knowable self that could be discovered and connected to, or participate in, a higher truth. With the emergence of the concept of existentialism and self-actualization, however, people no longer believed in an objective self. Instead, the self was seen as a construct invented through the choices individuals make and the lifestyles they adopt. Choice rather than wisdom is now the highest good, and freedom has largely been reduced to the idea of unfettered personal choice without unnecessary societal interference. We are free to be whoever we want to be.

It must be stressed, however, that both self-knowledge and self-invention are goals for only the happy few. While Christianity has held that self-knowledge comes chiefly through prayer and is, therefore, available even to the uneducated, in reality it has been largely pursued by those who could avail themselves of the philosophical education and leisure that provide the intellectual environment for pursuing truth. During the Middle Ages, the vast bulk of European society did not have the opportunity to pursue philosophical wisdom and self-knowledge. Similarly, self-invention is only available to those both affluent enough to have real economic choice and fortunate enough to be born in a culture that allows wide scope for pluralism and individuality. In other words, even in the twenty-first century most people in the world have little or no opportunity to rise beyond the situation into which they are born. Indeed, many of these people are now locked in wretched lives working to provide the affluent with the means to actualize their inner selves.

One fundamental difference between the ideas of self-knowledge and self-invention, however, is the place of the individual within society. In the pre-modern world, the 'social self' – the idea that I am who I am only because of various relationships that have shaped and continue to shape me – was an integral part of achieving self-knowledge. And because self-knowledge was connected with absolute truth, true knowledge of oneself was expressed in terms of a common set of virtues to which individuals aspired. Though the social pursuit of self-knowledge might be conducted in many different ways – the Greek academy or medieval monastery are just two examples – within Christianity it was typically expressed by the belief that only through learning to love God, neighbour and self properly can one really 'know thyself'. At least from the time of Augustine of Hippo, love was considered an essential part of understanding and, indeed, the highest form of knowledge. By contrast, self-creation (which has roots in the American ideal of 'self-reliance') has typically been cast in terms of the individual set against society. If I may create my own unique identity then there is every chance that my identity will have few connections with my neighbour's; in fact, it is entirely possible that my neighbour's self-invention may interfere and limit my own. So, individual self-interest has to be protected in order to provide the freedom for self-invention. Some, such as Robert Reich, a former member of Bill Clinton's administration, have pointed out that the logical conclusion of the self-invention movement is that society does not really exist but is only a fragmented mass of individuals.[7] From the other end of the political spectrum, Margaret Thatcher once famously stated that there is no such thing as society. Thus, whereas classical philosophers might believe in a whole series of obligations (to family, nation, truth, etc.) that are essential to happiness, self-actualizing individuals are only obliged to themselves; even those who rail against all forms of obligations will often promote their view with the phrase, 'You owe it to yourself'.

People quickly discovered, however, that having the freedom to self-create is altogether different from having the means to do so. Drawing from the new psychology of self-expression and influenced in part by such groups as the Human Potential Movement, economists and psychologists together popularized and expanded the concept of lifestyles.[8] The commonplace use of the term 'lifestyle' emerged partially through the wide influence of a study conducted in the 1970s by a research institute based at Stanford University, which determined that we are not nearly as infinitely creative as we like to think. In fact, people tend to 'self-create' themselves into a very limited number of behavioural patterns; these patterns are what we call lifestyles. Whereas before American society had been categorized demographically (gender, race, class, ethnicity, education), the new studies determined that 'self-actualizing' people could be more fundamentally categorized psychographically into lifestyles based on interests, activities and opinions. Fascinatingly, these categories seemed more predictive of behaviour than even class and race. At a subconscious level, we 'own' these identities more than we do the more apparent ones – like race and class – measured by demographers. Psychographics now plays an important role in political polling.

Once people could be classified into consumer lifestyles (coincidentally at the same moment that computers and robotics increased production exponentially) it was relatively simple to begin marketing products that would appeal to these various groups. Corporations developed focus groups that used psychographic techniques to explore the subconscious of the members of various lifestyles to determine how best to connect them emotionally with their products and brands; consequently, their products became emblematic for those lifestyles. Status symbols, once available only to the wealthiest, were popularized and made an essential part of everyone's identity. So, at the very time that most people had the opportunity to invent themselves they were given access to an ever-changing variety of clothing, music, diets, entertainment and other products for their consumption. Remarkably, almost all these choices were advertisements in themselves: brands were emblazoned on clothing, musicians were used to promote 'coolness' based on consumption, and lifestyle magazines, films, games and television were used as vehicles for additional advertisement. By the mid-1980s it had become impossible for anyone to avoid a persistent form of marketing that entered the privacy of the home as readily as it did the public domain.[9]

The emergence of the personal computer, laptops, the Internet and finally smart phones has greatly empowered corporations to connect their products with lifestyles and to produce a constant and increasingly individualized stream of advertising. For example, Google's ability to monitor individual interests and tailor advertising to those interests is the reason for its tremendous success. Instead of the persistent state propaganda envisioned by George Orwell in *1984*, we have advertising as the most common form of communication used today. As a result, part of modern life is navigating through a forest of advertising, which we do almost entirely subconsciously. The sales pitch, for most of human history rarely heard outside the market square, is one of the most common forms of expression that we now process or try to ignore.

The reason why Western society has so readily and profoundly bought into the idea of lifestyles is twofold. First, self-invention and lifestyle are inherently about identity. We want to individuate ourselves, to achieve a unique identity that we consider to be 'authentic'. Almost from the cradle, we are taught that by achieving this self-constructed identity we will finally obtain an otherwise elusive happiness. But the whole Western economic model is built on the assumption that the process of self-invention is interminable; there is always something about ourselves that we believe, or can be made to believe, needs perfecting or expressing. Is there really any identity we could ever construct that someone else could not deconstruct? The answer is no, and marketers know this. In fact, because the brands we use are constantly improved and reinvented, we assume the same thing about our own identity. We end up with two conflicting impulses: to find happiness in an authentic identity but never for long to accept any identity as truly authentic. In order to satisfy both impulses, we constantly look for products to help express our ever-changing identity and goals. In the process, we spend money and consume goods at an unsustainable rate, stripping the planet of its resources, locking millions in poverty and enriching a few.

The other reason why 'lifestyle marketing' is so effective is that one of the most powerful and most easily manipulated drives is desire. As Augustine recognized in the *Confessions*, the heart is restless, constantly pursuing the happiness it constantly craves. But this desire is often difficult to control. We rarely consider rationally what might actually make us happy, and even if we do, more often than not we find ourselves incapable of pursuing that course for long. Traditionally, this has led to the conclusion that we have a 'darker' nature, a less developed part of our self that resists reason and gives rise to unruly impulses. Plato referred to it as a wild horse, St Paul as the 'outer man', and Freud as the id. Moreover, our desires are conditioned by circumstances, conversations, families, education and many other unchosen and often forgotten influences. And so we frequently find that unsought pleasures spring upon us without really understanding why they do so. Just as tellingly, there are any number of ideas and interests we have intended to adopt but because they have not engaged our hearts (no matter how hard we have tried) they have never become habitual.

My sense of 'self' is, therefore, influenced by a mixture of all sorts of competing desires (many of them conflicting) that shape the way I lead and view my life. Many of my most cherished desires arose from a number of untraceable influences (not to mention the temperament with which I was born). Were I to begin to categorize these desires, I might be surprised by what I discovered, but I would also probably not be willing to do much about them. After all, I feel pleasure when they are occasionally satisfied; in many cases, the pursuit of the pleasure itself is desirable. I might perhaps relinquish a particular desire if the means of achieving it prove too costly or if a stronger desire should present itself. So, for example, many people have reduced the amount of television they watch only because they have more fun surfing the Internet or playing console games. All of this can be expressed simply: we want to be free to do as we please, but we have little control over what actually pleases us. And this is where consumerism finds its foothold in the human psyche.

Commerce and the drive for self-actualization create a fertile environment in which our desires can be subconsciously manipulated by marketing. Corporations have become incredibly adept at influencing our desires and pleasures. From a very young age, we are conditioned to desire an ever-changing array of products and services. But, conversely, the system also works by keeping us perpetually dissatisfied with what we have and own; therefore, our attention remains fixed on what we lack, be it goods, personal qualities or the secure happiness we forever pursue. William Cavanaugh observes that this gives rise to a new form of greed based not on undue attachment to things but on detachment from them:

> Most people are not overly attached to things, and most are not obsessed with hoarding riches ... What really characterizes consumer culture is not attachment to things but detachment. People do not hoard money; they spend it. People do not cling to things; they discard them and buy other things.[10]

This detachment suspends us in a state of desire, and our time and money are spent in accumulating 'new' things, not so much to add to our treasury of goods as to replace those things we consider obsolete or no longer appealing. Cavanaugh notes further: 'Consumerism is not so much about having more as it is about having something else; that's why it is not simply *buying* but *shopping* that is the heart of consumerism.'[11] And the constant appeal to shop that comes through programmes, commercials, music and film shapes the way we view ourselves.

Perhaps one of the most telling examples of the manipulation of desire is the expansion of computer and console gaming among men. According to a survey conducted by the Entertainment Software Association, the average age of a gamer is now 37, a segment of the population who 20 years ago hardly played such games.[12] Almost a third of gamers are over 50. Computers, the Internet and mobiles have provided marketers with a veritable cornucopia of products to sell. Games, gadgets and applications can be produced at an astonishing rate and made available to a worldwide audience (still largely composed of men) of all ages, classes and cultures. And within this virtual world, desire is readily manipulated: people always want to have their gaming experiences improved, expanded and enriched, which leads not only to new games but to new computers and gadgets capable of handling better graphics and gameplay. These, in turn, create a market for associated books and magazines, derivative films and novels, associated music and imagery, and to a whole host of other products to support a lifestyle built around gaming. Today, we have a multibillion-dollar industry that hardly existed 30 years ago.

The emergence of the gaming lifestyle highlights another influence on desire and identity: the need to fit in. Even though self-invention is all about defining ourselves free from societal pressures, in reality we always feel the urge to be accepted by our peers. Thus we may find ourselves desiring a lifestyle or an interest simply because it is part of the dominant culture in which we live. We worry about the influence of peer pressure on our children and teens, even while we 'try to keep up with the Joneses'. But our need to feel accepted is also essential to consumerism: without it, there could be no fashions. Absurdly, most of us seem to have the need to express our individuality in the same way everybody else does. This is why, despite the deep impact of self-invention, Western society has been reduced not to a chaotic soup of uniquely expressed individuals but to a slightly less chaotic and often competing collection of identifiable lifestyles called consumer tribes.[13]

The centrality of consumerism to our identity has consequently generated an astonishing sense of entitlement. We feel entitled to all the goods we desire, and we have ready access to credit in order to live a lifestyle we otherwise cannot afford. As a result, one of the most identifiable features of consumerism is consumer debt. Many pundits may have pointed to the ways in which the 2011 London riots were rooted in consumerism, but we are all like those youths who raided shops for shoes, clothing, televisions and mobiles. We demand the latest mobiles, televisions, gadgetry and fashionable clothing at prices that are unsustainable in the long term and even now are deeply destructive to the societies and the environment in which they are produced. We may not riot in order to enjoy all these products, but we deprive developing countries of their resources and political well-being in order to satisfy our own desires. And it is becoming increasingly clear that the world cannot long sustain our excessive levels of consumption.

People, of course, do not generally want others to suffer. But we are detached from the sources of production and, therefore, not compelled to think about the origin of our goods. Detachment, whether from production, the goods themselves, the natural world or from one another is a characteristic feature of consumerism. Because we emphasize our own self-invention apart from society, consumption apart from production, products apart from a cultural context, and (increasingly) technological communication apart from face-to-face relationships, we become isolated from the world. One result of this detachment is that we find ourselves living in communities where, because there is now no shared personal history (as we probably did not grow up with our neighbours) and little by way of shared local culture, the bonds that hold communities together are collapsing. Any given neighbourhood or village will contain a variety of lifestyles that may separate neighbours from each other because their commitments, interests and pleasures do not interconnect. With the closing of local gathering places such as pubs and churches, neighbours may not even know each other except for the bare recognition that comes from glimpsing each other briefly when driving elsewhere or doing outdoor chores. All of this can lead to a sense of tremendous isolation and an impoverishment of any sense of home.

To avoid this sense of isolation and dislocation, we have developed into a society of 'networks' whereby we use primarily technological means (cars, mobiles, television and, above all else, the Internet) to connect with people whose lifestyle approximates or intersects with our own. Society is now 'fragmented' into gathered communities or consumer tribes bound together by shared information and technology rather than by a shared locality.[14] By and large, these networks rely on corporations for their existence (car manufacturers, Twitter, Facebook, etc.) and are focused on forms of consumption (such as music groups, diet, fashion), which keep individual identity locked into consumerism. Because they are not embedded in any particular place, networks are typically very fluid: one may be simultaneously part of any number of other ever-changing networks and move freely between them. They do provide a common culture of a kind that is typically based on a shared lifestyle or form of consumption with the apparent benefit that one may opt in or out as one chooses. Indeed, most people move from network to network as their own interests, lifestyle and circumstances change. When this happens, bonds of mutual affection do not so much break as slowly wither without undue rancour. We simply 'move on' with life, an idea that suggests not so much maturation as a change in interests or primary identity. We call this a 'change of lifestyle', a term that is morally neutral; changing lifestyles is no worse than switching brands.

Network cultures also differ from traditional cultures in the way that they are communicated over time. Traditional cultures are generally conveyed through elders handing down traditions to the young both through family and local traditions and education. This grounds collective and individual identities in both place and time; this enables the past to speak to the present. In other words, a geographically based environment is shaped by a history, shared experience, traditions and local loyalties. Of course, the organic transmission of culture still happens, not least through shared language, but now this 'handing down' is in stiff competition with a free-floating, technological culture disseminated through various forms of commercial media. In fact, one no longer really thinks of being educated into a particular culture – that sounds too elitist – but of having the freedom to choose whatever lifestyle and to engage in whatever networks one wishes within a global, digital ecosystem.

The transmission of culture through commerce is not necessarily questionable or even novel. During the Middle Ages, society was profoundly influenced by the Eastern trade that the Crusades inadvertently encouraged. Colonial trade with the New World and the European colonies enabled entirely foreign cultures to enrich European art and culture. One has only to consider how the introduction of West Indian sugar and Chinese tea into England shaped British society from the seventeenth century onwards. But thanks to the omnipresence of advertising and the immediacy of other cultures through the mass media, the communication of culture through commerce is on a scale previously inconceivable. Moreover, instead of just providing the means for sharing ideas and practices, global commerce now creates its own disembedded environment in which individuals can enjoy together various marketed products. Participation in a consumer tribe that is disembedded from any particular place or culture is the common denominator that shapes participating individual identities. In reality, the shared environment is an independent space accessed from anywhere in the world. The impact of these shared spaces, entirely mediated through the marketplace and typically branded, may so shape the way individuals think of themselves that their local cultures become little more than an ethnic flavouring of their consumer identity. Their world of meaning is drawn mainly from what is now styled the 'digital ecosystem'; where they feel most connected to someone else is in their particular style of shared consumption.

This may explain why the Information Age appears to encourage a flattening out of cultural identities; instead of a flourishing of culture, societies are increasingly rationalized in accordance with consumerist principles: the homogenized shopping centres and districts and the uniform housing that characterize our built environments. One may now travel the world over and discover sprawling estates of look-alike homes laid out in identical fashion or walk down the High Street in almost any prosperous nation and find many of the same shops exhibiting their wares under the same signs and employing identical management techniques. Public space has become *de*territorialized.[15] Indeed, except for the continuing (though ever-shrinking) barrier of languages, one can move from country to country without having to abandon many of the goods one has customarily enjoyed.

This 'McDonaldization' of society is usually presented as hip and cosmopolitan.[16] Even in an age when many people grow suspicious of globalization and embrace the (ironically global) message 'Think locally', regional customs are considered old-fashioned, 'uncool' or, in some cases, elitist. How many cultural movements of the past 50 years have set a new practice or taste promoted by corporations against those embedded within local societies? This presents itself most clearly with music and fashion where the 'bold' and 'creative' are almost always those who draw from global influences to break down traditional tastes and resist cultural expectations. The movie *Footloose* embodies this feature of consumerism. While overtly the movie is about young people standing up for their individual freedoms against the oppression of right-wing religion, implicitly it is about the victory of consumer culture over a traditional one. After all, the lifestyle, music and fashion embraced by Kevin Bacon's lead character and his friends are those promoted by corporations worldwide and not ones they have created themselves. Their self-expression is really nothing more than the embrace of commercial media culture. For all the individualism championed in the film, in reality the youth are choosing the new, 'cool' culture over the local one. Freedom really amounts to little more than their choosing to be defined by another culture every bit as collectivizing as the one they are rejecting. If *Footloose* were re-scripted to present a local community seeking to prevent corporations from destroying its culture for their own profit one would end up with *Avatar*. What makes the film work is that we the audience by and large share Kevin Bacon's consumerized world.

Finally, both the fervency with which we have embraced consumerism and the damage that consumerism is causing to culture, societies and the planet demonstrate why the ideas of self-invention, absolute free choice and lifestyle cannot be sustained for long. During the 1980s and 1990s, critics of consumerism were largely cast as Luddites, cranks or religious moralists. There seemed to be no reason other than some outmoded religious scrupulosity to deny oneself the plenitude of riches that consumerism offers. As long as everyone has the freedom to be whatever they want to be, does it really matter if a few are disproportionately enriched in the process? During the Internet boom of the 1990s, we even began to believe that we had developed a perfect economic system that could somehow indefinitely feed excess while generating enormous profits from that excess.

Ironically, globalism and the technology that engendered such optimism have also made us more mindful of the costs of self-invention and the so-called freedom of consumer choice. First, we are increasingly conscious of environmental damage (such as toxic rivers and wastelands, global warming and accumulating plastic waste) that consumerism inflicts on our natural world. We now know that the world simply cannot support its entire population consuming resources at the same rate as Westerners do; subsequently, arguments about environmental sustainability are now a major part of public discourse. Second, the shocking experience of the financial crises that began in 2001 and blew up into a clear threat to the colossal financial sector in 2008 has made most people aware of the fragility of our economic system. Even in the face of severe environmental degradation, however, we seem to want to have our cake and eat it: we are working hard to find renewable ways to sustain our level of consumption even as we swiftly develop new practices to exploit energy and resources. Few speak seriously of reducing levels of consumption. How can they when frugality on a massive level would restrict the revenues whereby governments support research into renewable energy and sustainability? We are trapped in a nightmare where our need to slim down depends on our capacity to overindulge.

Another reason why consumerism ought to be resisted is that we can only enjoy its fruits because the vast majority of the world's population cannot. Ultimately, the enjoyment in wealthy nations of maximized choice, self-actualization and ready access to goods and services is based on profound inequality. The majority of the world has to remain locked in economic servitude, often enduring severe environmental and political degradation so that global companies produce cheaply the goods required for the rest of us to pursue the kind of lives to which we believe ourselves entitled. That remains the cruel and enduring irony of our consumer identity: we are only free to be who we want to be because almost everybody else is not. That is the sad and often hidden consequence of our reliance on cheap consumer goods. But in order to see our dependency on consumerism more clearly, we must now look at how consumerism shapes our lives from the moment we are born.

2

Initiation into consumerism

————◆•◆•◆————

Initiation into the Christian faith involves two rites: baptism and confirmation. Baptism is the sacrament whereby one is incorporated into the body of Christ and begins life as a Christian. Within liturgical Christianity, baptism is ideally followed at a later age by the rite of confirmation when individuals profess their baptismal vows for themselves and embark upon their Christian adulthood. Similarly, although the initiation of people into consumerism is more of a process than an event, it can be divided into two stages: in the first stage young children are 'baptized' into consumerism and firmly grounded in its world-view; in the second stage they engage as adolescents actively with consumer culture to develop an identity and an understanding of the world. Together these two stages provide the emotional and intellectual environment in which the initiated relate to one another, understand and weigh issues, and experience the underlying pattern of their own lives.

The baptism into consumerism: commercialization of childhood

During the 1970s in the USA, a disparate collection of activists began to worry about the expanding role of marketing in children's lives. Eventually, advocacy groups petitioned the Federal Trade Commission (FTC) to consider imposing various levels of restrictions on advertising to children.[1] In the midst of these discussions, however, Congress passed the Federal Trade Commission Improvement Act, which removed from the FTC any authority to regulate marketing to children.[2] Subsequently, children's marketing grew at an astonishing rate, so that by 2006 US children were spending $40 billion and influencing the additional spending of $700 billion a year.[3] As with adults, the lives of children changed dramatically within a very brief period.

Although the UK and the European Union have maintained much stricter regulations about marketing to children, advertising made similar inroads into children's lives in Europe during the same period. The arrival of MTV, a channel devoted entirely to lifestyle marketing, is an obvious benchmark of this development. The advent of the Internet has made it even more difficult for regulators to limit the exposure of children to advertising now featured on websites, mobiles, online entertainment and games. So, it should be no surprise that despite regulations, the children and teenage market in the UK has grown to an astonishing £30 billion a year.[4] Indeed, according to a report by the Institute for Public Policy Research, evidence suggests that in the UK children are now more 'enmeshed' in consumerism than children in the US.[5]

Of course, marketing to children is not a new development. Since at least the late nineteenth century, businesses have recognized that money can be made from consumer products aimed at children. The impact of this is seen in the very way in which we conceive of childhood: 'toddler', 'tween' and 'teenager' are all terms developed by the commercial world to help identify or create focused markets for their goods and services. With the expansion of television ownership, followed by the introduction of computers, the Internet and mobiles, however, the opportunities and dimensions of such marketing have vastly expanded. *Teletubbies, Elmo, Bratz, Power Rangers, Dora the Explorer*, and any number of other brand products, influence or define the play of children through their pervasive role in children's imaginative and sensual world. The age at which brand marketing begins has also been brought forward. Even items that are necessary for infants and toddlers (for example, dummies, sippy cups, nappies, toys and bedding) come with logos and characters created to draw their attention and lay the foundation for brand loyalty. One recent study determined that reception-age children can typically identify a large number of brands and even 'willingly judge their peers' according to brand use.[6] A study in 2003 of children first entering school found that while only half of them could recognize their own name, speak articulately or count to five, 81 per cent of them could recognize the Coca-Cola logo and 69 per cent the McDonald's golden arches.[7] Thus, before children have a chance even to begin developing a sense of self, they have been locked into a consumer world; once they are put in front of the television or computer, there is really no turning back.

Children play three roles for marketers. First, they are consumers, though the overall market potential for children under 13 is still limited. A much more vital part of the economy, however, is their second role as influencers of adult purchasing. Corporate strategists realize that 'a great deal of younger children's consumption is in fact parents' consumption'.[8] Marketers, therefore, cleverly develop their pitches to encourage children to 'nag' or 'pester' their parents into buying various brands. Known in the USA as the 'nag factor' and in the UK (where it is regulated) as 'pester power', this marketing strategy encourages children to demand products from their parents. Finally, children present marketers with long-term market potential: the motto for this is 'cradle to grave' brand loyalty. Although fast-food and soft-drink companies provide notorious examples of this kind of advertising, it was Apple that transformed this area of marketing for the digital age with its introduction of the iPod. Marketed as a 'cool', 'must-have' gadget, it quickly became something that even young children demanded. The pop stars fronting the iPod commercials made it almost irresistible, and parents were happy to oblige. Not only has this obviously increased sales of the iPod, but it has established extraordinary brand loyalty among buyers. The worldwide adulation of Steve Jobs upon his death illustrates this point well. More recently, mobile companies have developed a similar strategy, often playing on parental fear to encourage them to answer their children's demands.

As marketing has moved into children's lives, both public and private spaces have been commodified. Corporations sponsor sports teams and arenas, playgrounds, leisure grounds and school programmes, buildings and activities. Indeed, although the growing presence of marketing in education has caused heated debate, little has dissuaded companies from pursuing a captive audience on school grounds. The impact of consumerism on education is generally divided into two strategies: *endogeneous* and *exogeneous*. Endogeneous strategies refer to the importation of private-sector, largely business-derived, techniques into the educational sector in order to make the running and management of schools reflect corporate culture and to attract corporate funding. Exogeneous strategies involve the importation of commercial advertising directly into the schools.[9] Both strategies either directly or indirectly transform schools into commercial environments.[10]

The report on the impact of commercialization indicates three other forms of commodification in childhood: family time, fear and safety. The report states:

> there is much greater pressure on parents to spend time with their children – and indeed to be seen to enjoy doing so. In this context, one could argue that the notion of 'quality time' spent with children has itself been commodified – that is, seen as something that can be bought and sold. Parents may use purchases as a way of compensating for the feelings of guilt they experience as a result of not spending what they are led to regard as sufficient time with their children – even though the figures suggest that they are in fact spending more time on childcare than previous generations of parents. Indeed, studies of the marketing of toys suggest that commercial goods for children are often promoted in precisely this manner.[11]

Next, marketers play on parental fears to promote a perception that domestic use of media is safer than unsupervised play outdoors. As a result, bedrooms are becoming 'media-rich' environments. Finally, 'safety spaces' are commodified: the shopping centre is a good example of a commodified public space where children are left without overt adult supervision. Additionally, a growing number of leisure areas – such as playgrounds and sporting facilities – are being funded and managed by companies who also fund organized sports programmes that draw increasing numbers of children.

Clearly, children cannot easily avoid marketing, and because they absorb the images and messages of advertising during their most impressionable age, their understanding of themselves and their world is dramatically influenced by consumerism. Brands become a part of their growing sense of identity. The Institute for Public Policy Research's report, *Freedom's Orphans*, concludes that:

> children are becoming more dependent on brands to give them a sense of the aspirations, values, and possessions that are important and acceptable – that brands are beginning to powerfully dictate social hierarchies in a way formerly done by communities and parents, effectively making judgements of value about what is appropriate in terms of lifestyle and normative behaviour.[12]

In other words, the lifestyle marketing that was originally aimed at adult consumers now also develops children as consumers; marketers are effectively grooming children to be loyal customers of particular brands.

The commodification of childhood also means that young children are introduced to a global market before they have any capacity to cope with it. That global market becomes their world; their exposure to television, film, popular music and the Internet far outweighs in time and attention the impact of any local or traditional culture. This 'new digital ecosystem' is where children, even from a very early age, spend much of their leisure time, and marketers see this ecosystem as an environment of almost limitless advertising potential.[13] Similarly, the fictional characters with whom young children relate are typically creations of the market, and the subjects that interest them most are those that appear on television or in games. For example, in many households, various worlds created by Disney to sell products shape children's earliest lives and provide them with shared memories and interests. Hannah Montana is a good example of a celebrity aimed at a tween. *Star Wars* is another example of a world created solely for profit – George Lucas notoriously described himself as a toymaker who shoots films – which becomes the 'culture' in which children imaginatively live and play. Visit almost any toy shop and you will be hard pressed to find any goods that are not related to a character from a television programme, console game or film. Consequently, a few global corporations are shaping the imagination and play of millions of children worldwide.

This point illustrates a defining irony of consumerism. Even while it claims to promote individuality, it compels conformity through the virtual and imaginary worlds it creates. As children strive through play and narrative to find their place in the world, they are not given freedom to enjoy their own imagination, drawing from their experience of family, neighbours, friends and their natural environment. They are not even raised within a particular, organic culture. Instead, they are provided with a limited range of imaginary worlds – such as Disney, *Star Wars*, *Harry Potter*, various superheroes, and anime creations like *Pokémon* – that they explore through film, television, games and products, which do much of the imaginary work for them. In fact, their play is less a form of imagination than of mimicry; they are re-enacting what they have seen on the screen. While some of these creations can be enormously complex and evocative – particularly those like *Harry Potter*, which have only become widely marketed through toys and films after their initial success – they are all part of a single digital environment that has become the overriding culture in which they live, relate to each other and develop values. Thus, beginning with Disney cartoons, *Teletubbies*, *Sesame Street* and *Thomas the Tank Engine* (among others), children become dependent on an imaginary life that is incarnated through products and media.

That imaginary world also tends either to be intolerant of traditional cultures or to co-opt them within a consumer framework. One will rarely find overtly religious or ethnic customs presented in storylines; when they are, it is typically as part of a theme of tolerance. But as children grow older, traditional norms and religious and ethnic customs that limit access to the world of consumerism are subtly undermined. Such cultures may be tolerated, but they are definitely not 'cool'. Members of those cultures are, therefore, depicted as intolerant, backward, crude and, above all else, boring. For example, in the animated movie *Happy Feet*, the priestly caste of elder penguins (whose leader is portrayed as a kind of dour Presbyterian minister) attempts to prevent the main character from expressing his true self. To avoid such characterization, various micro-cultures package, market and commodify themselves for a targeted segment of society. One of the most positive depictions of Roman Catholicism, for example, is *Sister Act*, in which a convent of rather staid nuns becomes more appealing by embracing Whoopi Goldberg's 'hipper' form of music. To preserve themselves, traditional cultures such as religions are pressured to translate how they express themselves into ways more acceptable to consumer culture.

Often, however, an overtly antagonistic approach to traditional cultures will be seen as insensitive, and so marketers and media corporations deliberately co-opt them into a consumerist framework. Disney most notably introduced this tactic as early as the 1930s with its animated adaptation of traditional fairy tales. Walt Disney openly expressed his belief that the films ought not to be bound by the original stories; *Sleeping Beauty* and *The Jungle Book* are notable examples of this. Similarly, most children who love Winnie the Pooh are familiar with only Disney's depiction of him; many have never read the original books by A. A. Milne. Perhaps worse, however, is Disney's use of cultural stories as commercial vehicles for a set of values, products, theme parks and food. Films such as *Aladdin*, *Pocahontas* and *Mulan*, while ostensibly multicultural, do little justice to the cultures they represent or to the classical stories they purport to retell. In fact, the characters and storylines are interchangeable because they are not really situated in any particular culture: their purpose is not to instil or portray a set of cultural norms but to sell an array of products. All of this could be dismissed as benign entertainment were it not, again, for the way they permeate children's lives. These and other similar stories have become the wellsprings of imagination for millions of children. Any classical story or fairy tale not adapted and popularized by film and ancillary products is soon forgotten. In the end, even traditional cultures are commodified.

The consumer world of children is also enormously stimulating. Children are bombarded with loud sounds, bright colours and rapid scene changes that hyper-stimulate the brain. Indeed, research has shown that the stimulation of television and computer games at a young age rewires the brain so that it becomes addicted to a high level of stimulation; it craves rapidity of movement in the same ways that those accustomed to sweet foods crave sugar.[14] This rewiring will undoubtedly become even more profound as scientists learn more about how the brain functions and responds to stimuli. Without regulation, advertising may soon become almost irresistible, affecting us in ways we cannot knowingly resist.[15]

The pervasive commercialization of childhood introduces a central paradox of consumerism. While it purports to create a world in which individuals have an almost infinite and unfettered range of choices, it actually limits choice from a very early age. It is only because children are socialized as consumers that they may embark on a life of self-invention through consumption. Any expression of individualism from that point onwards will be expressed within a consumerist framework. Few reach adolescence in a neutral state in which they may freely choose to become consumers. By the time children reach the age at which they have the capacity for critical thought, they know of no other way of being; consumerism has profoundly shaped the way they see themselves and their society. According to the 'Children and Marketing Literature' report:

> Today's children and young people are growing up in a cultural
> environment which is becoming more saturated with promotional

messages than ever before. They are persistently encouraged to think of themselves as consumers. We need to ask whether this has consequences for education in citizenship, designed to encourage a rising generation to think of themselves as members of a moral and political community and to see their future as inextricably linked to the quality of public life.[16]

This situation is deeply ironic: parents who feel strongly about deferring baptism or discussing religion because they want their children to be free to decide for themselves happily bring up their children to be thoroughgoing consumers.[17] But this simply supports the claim that consumerism is best understood as a religion. Parents are comfortable with their children's baptism into consumerism because it is their own way of life.

Adolescence: the confirmation of a consumer

Until recently, the Western Church taught that the sacrament of confirmation was the completion of the grace received at baptism. While few theologians still hold this view, the old understanding of confirmation does provide a useful analogy for the next stage in the development of the consumer: adolescence. During the teenage years, when boys and girls wrestle with their own identity and place in the world, the consumerist mindset is fully developed and solidified. Indeed, so successful is the establishment of a consumer identity during people's teenage years that they rarely emerge from it. Perhaps nothing better illustrates this than the astonishing longevity of computer gaming as a pastime well into mature adulthood. In fact, there is now a new category developing to identify people (especially men) in their twenties and thirties: pre-adulthood.[18] Nor should the success of consumerism among adolescents be surprising. The promise that one may invent an identity through consumption and in the face of societal pressures accords well with the instinctive, adolescent urge to separate from one's parents in the pursuit of independence. Consumerism provides teenagers with a dazzling array of choices to distinguish themselves from their elders. Thus, the teenager is one who has begun to 'own' his or her consumer identity just as a confirmand is one who has begun to 'own' his or her Christian identity.

'Own' is probably the wrong term here, however, since the whole structure of 'youth culture' is constructed to give teenagers only the illusion of 'owning' their own identity in order to create markets. Billions of dollars have been spent identifying what exactly pleases teenagers so that product-based lifestyles can be promoted. These lifestyles are the norm towards which teenagers are drawn through the appeal of fun and happiness; marketers define the 'coolness' that teenagers crave to possess in order to stand out from the crowd. Thus 'coolness' is not their own invented 'culture' but one that is presented repeatedly in television, film, music and magazines and that builds upon the media-based stories and identities of their childhood.

Whereas confirmation introduces Christians to their journey towards holiness, the advent of adolescence introduces consumers to the frenzied pursuit of 'coolness'. Both the Christian and consumerist ideals play very similar roles, providing an ever-elusive goal that keeps people running the race that is set before them. Neither the Christian nor the consumer ever achieves perfection (however defined) in this life. Also, in neither case do individuals define that goal themselves; holiness is defined by Scripture and the Church, and coolness by a combination of music, fashion and style influenced by marketing and advertising. In that sense, both sanctification and coolness describe processes whereby people strive for a common ideal. The Book of Common Prayer memorably describes holiness by pointing us towards Jesus 'in whose service is perfect freedom' – similarly, teenagers gain a sense of boundless freedom through their willing service to a culture of coolness and style.

A recent television advertisement illustrates this point. In the commercial, a then popular music star briefly escapes during the intermission of her concert by riding a bike to a local convenience shop. She launches into a song about living a life that's more than mere survival that climaxes with the refrain, 'I've gotta be free . . . I gotta be me.' She cycles around the shop aisles a few times before making her way back to the concert. In the meantime, her singing brings smiles to a woman shopping and a car full of girls putting on make-up, before she arrives back, happy and refreshed, to entertain her adoring fans. What induces this brief act of freedom? A few sips from a soft drink. The advertisement almost perfectly represents the constant sermon of consumerism preached to teenagers: freedom and the fullness of life are found through consumption. And by showing the star cycling boldly around the aisles of a shop, the advertisement sends the message that her act, though sweet and charming, is a kind of rebellion without any consequences: even the cashier smiles at her stunt.

One can, of course, make light of the commercial or point out that it is unlikely to make young men and women run out to purchase a soft drink in order to embrace personal freedom. But the ubiquity of this message is very difficult to ignore. It is part of a constant chorus transmitted through songs, magazines, television shows, films, commercials, the Internet and games that conveys one powerful message to teenagers: in order to be yourself you have to be cool. The amazing thing is that our youth never seem to grow tired of the message. There is something irresistible about the idea that by listening to the right bands, wearing the right clothes and engaging in the right activities one will somehow defy society and enjoy the freedom of individuality, even though all this is expressed through images of people acting alike. The idea that individualism can be discovered and expressed through group conformity is certainly an odd cultural phenomenon.

Of course, coolness itself is in the eye of the beholder and over time manifests itself in many different ways. That is part of its allure because once anything cool is perceived to have become too mainstream, it ceases to be cool. Coolness requires a degree of edginess that gives it remarkable energy as it seeks new ways to distinguish itself from sanctioned cultures. One of the tricks of successful marketers is to promote a lifestyle without seeming to do so. Despite (or perhaps because of) their immersion in consumerism from a young age, many teenagers react negatively to overt manipulation by marketers. One can see this in television advertisements: those aimed at children lack subtlety, declaring, 'Buy this because it's cool.' But that does not work with teenagers. Instead, corporations carefully place their products in scenes that present a lifestyle that their research has shown to be trendy. Often, nothing in the advert actually informs the viewer about the product itself; the message is simply that it belongs in or is a sign of that cool subculture.

Despite the elusive quality of coolness, masculine and feminine stereotypes have broadly endured or have been exaggerated. On the one hand, films, programmes and videos aimed at young men frequently present 'cool' masculinity as boorish, crude and reckless yet somehow the object of female attention. The teenage male's life is devoted to heavy drinking, parties, music and destructive behaviours, and his manhood is demonstrated by both his ability to give himself entirely over to these activities and his sexual prowess. This image is a carefully constructed montage of qualities that extensive focus group analysis and interviews have determined will appeal strongly to a wide segment of the teenage, male population.[19] He frequently appears on channels such as MTV, in shows like *Jackass*, in any number of commercials and music videos, and in films such as *The Hangover* and *American Pie*. On the other hand, the stereotype directed at young women presents 'cool' young women as overtly sexual, preoccupied with shopping and designer goods, willing to conform to male expectations, and finding self-worth through their attraction of 'cool' males. As with the male stereotype, the teenage 'nymphette' is a product of focus groups and interviews with young women. And it is almost impossible to ignore her ubiquity: she is in many ways the standard-bearer of contemporary consumerism, manifested in such people as Rihanna and Britney Spears, and in innumerable doctored images in magazines, on hoardings and Internet sites, and in film.

In his fascinating *Frontline* documentary, 'Merchants of Cool', Douglas Rushkoff shows how these stereotypes are carefully constructed through intensive focus group research by corporations.[20] From their own perspective, these corporations are simply using psychological techniques to discover what teenagers really desire. To an extent, this is undoubtedly true and part of their attraction to teens. But the corporations are ultimately interested only in what sells, and so they choose to emphasize only those aspects of adolescence that their research suggests will sell products. Rushkoff argues that the whole relationship between teenagers and corporations in determining 'coolness' is like a feedback loop. Corporations use their analysis of teenagers to create images and ideas for a 'cool' lifestyle in which to situate their products. But many teenagers realize that corporations are doing this, and some of them behave so as to attract the attention of corporate researchers. From this loop emerges a marketed 'cool' culture that becomes normative. In order to stand out from this new normative 'coolness', teenagers must then behave even more outlandishly in order to attract attention; this then, when studied, creates a new marketed image of edginess. Each manufactured lifestyle becomes one step further removed from normal adolescent life and the characteristics represented through the media become that much more cartoonish.

Increasingly, both gender stereotypes are reinforced by the emergence of a new pressure on teenagers: online pornography. Recent surveys in the UK suggest that teenagers spend more than an hour each week watching online pornography.[21] Although statistics such as these can always be questioned, obviously the availability of pornography through the Internet via laptops and mobiles has increased considerably during the past 20 years. Leaving aside for the moment moral questions about pornography, the very nature of the phenomenon promotes the stereotype of young women as sexual objects and of young men behaving badly. Marketers know the allure of pornography, and as a result there has been an undoubted coarsening of the types of sexual imagery openly aimed at young men and women. One of the messages common to all displays of sex is that it is primarily a form of entertainment, directed largely towards self-gratification, and normally without adverse consequences.

In fact, the freedom to embrace these lifestyles without consequences is a reason for their popularity. Not only does each lifestyle offer the hope of happiness through a purchased self-expression, but each also advertises itself as being completely unproblematic. Many critics have focused on such obvious examples of this as diet, alcohol consumption and sedentary lifestyle: teenagers are told that they can spend their time eating fast food, drinking soft drinks, imbibing large quantities of alcohol, engaging in promiscuous sexual activity and spending hours playing console games, and remain slim, fit, healthy and attractive. Rarely mentioned, however, is the unsustainability of this youth culture, not only in terms of finances, family cohesion and emotional well-being but also in terms of the global environment. Astonishing levels of energy, resources and labour are required to provide teenagers with their lifestyle choices, which, in turn, produce a mountain of waste. Our youth get to enjoy their lifestyles because the majority of the youth of this world cannot; neither production nor resources could long maintain such extravagance on a worldwide level. Unfortunately, however much authorities harp on about the true consequences of these youth consumer lifestyles to both society and individuals, they meet with either indifference or anger. In the end, they are ineffective because at the heart of youth culture is the act of rebellion; authorities simply advertise the kind of expectations against which teenagers rebel. It does not help matters that teenagers can see that the authorities themselves engage in much the same behaviour: older consumers lecturing younger consumers about their consumption is rarely convincing.

It would be absurd to suggest that all teenagers conform to these two stereotypes. Youth culture is composed of a colourful array of consumer tribes, each with its own defining characteristics. Almost all these subcultures, however, are creations of the marketing world – or, if not creations, then modified and popularized through marketing – that are either defined by various consumer products (music groups, clothing styles and leisure activities) or connected with specific brands (e.g. Abercrombie and Fitch, Adidas, and Gap). Much of teenage life involves navigating through the various subcultures in order to develop a sense of individual identity. Indeed, recent marketing research indicates that teenagers are becoming 'tribal tourists', flitting from one lifestyle to another without establishing a lasting loyalty to any particular group. The same report speaks excitedly about how this development shows that technology is 'giving teenagers the confidence to explore different groups and interests, pushing boundaries to express themselves'.[22] What the article fails to note is that the 'digital tools' by which teenagers do push boundaries and express themselves are developed, branded and maintained by global corporations. This digital world is also saturated with images and sound bites rather than face-to-face conversations and relationships. Increasingly, teenagers demonstrate that they belong to a certain lifestyle (however briefly) by advertising themselves as a tribal member through the brands they wear and the way they construct their social media pages.

Tellingly, many teenagers believe that the corporations that fabricate these scenes and images are the ones who really are listening to their desires. There is a pervasive sense that some corporations – Viacom's MTV is a good example – actually understand teenagers better than their own families. And, of course, they do, since they are interested not in what is best for teenagers but in what they want or, at least, what they think they want. A few desires – typically sex and recklessness – can be exaggerated and expanded through music videos, commercials and films to convince teenagers that someone understands what makes them feel happy and empowered. Another reason why the corporations can appear to be understanding is because they have already been long at work developing teenagers' desires and expectations; they are just confirming what was established during a child's baptism into consumerism. Thus, corporations operate within the culture the children know through their exposure to media and marketing from a young age. Indeed, their maturation has been charted by their movement from one level of programming to the next (for example, from *Teletubbies* to *Pokémon* to *Dr Who* to *Glee* to *Gossip Girls*).

The cult of coolness sets in place the networks and free-floating lifestyles that so characterize adult consumerism. During adolescence, young men and women enter into a culture that is not grounded in any particular ethnicity, region or tradition, and so can be packaged and carried with them wherever they go in life. Its life blood is the digital ecosystem that is accessible from any computer or mobile, viewed on countless channels and heard through millions of music devices from almost anywhere in the world. That digital culture is simply a development of the world in which their imaginative lives were formed in childhood. There is no longer any need to outgrow the cult of coolness; in fact, because it is the culture in which children and youth have been formed it is as difficult to leave that culture as it is for people to reject their ethnicity. To be a consumer, a member of the cult of coolness, is to be a citizen of the world. That is far more exciting than any traditional culture locked into a specific location and restricted by a limited number of customs.

That digital ecosystem, however, is as tribal as any traditional culture. Children and teenagers quickly learn to self-segregate themselves according to interests and lifestyle. Popular music has long been the vehicle for this tribalism, dividing teenagers into hippies, head bangers, punkers, mods, ravers, hip-hop, grunge and any number of other varieties of lifestyle. Each of these conforms to an image derived from products, styles and behaviour that can give individuals a powerful sense of identity and commonality. Today, such tribes are reinforced and mediated through the Internet, personal music devices and mobiles: teenagers have almost no need to emerge from their tribal world even when physically alone. Moreover, these networks of youth culture can be every bit as mutually antagonistic as traditional tribes. Integral to them all is not simply belonging but also rejecting. So, for example, in becoming avid fans of speed metal, teenagers also identify themselves against fans of pop music. Within youth culture, these divisions can often be incredibly intense and a cause of continual anxiety.[23]

The excesses of youth culture have become so apparent that parents, social groups and even politicians have grown ever more concerned about the pressures teenagers face and the values that they are imbibing. But, ironically, many of the initiatives developed to challenge the hyper-consumerism of youth culture depend similarly on consumerism. They borrow from the marketing world to try to popularize their ideas. Marketers are enlisted to help 'shape public opinion' by using precisely the same techniques employed to develop a culture of coolness only now to popularize healthier lifestyles. The campaign against tobacco use is a good example of this approach, especially in the way that it has sought to convince teenagers that smoking is uncool. A second approach involves identifying aspects of youth culture that meet with adult approval so they can be imbued with moral worth. The best example of this approach is sport: an activity that has been almost completely subsumed within consumer culture and yet is supported by millions of parents as a vehicle for promoting not just fitness but all sorts of moral values. Indeed, sport has arguably become the main arena for children's moral development, demonstrated by how many are engaged in recreational sports in comparison to those who attend religious services. Millions of teenagers devote much of their leisure time to organized, recreational sports funded by businesses, which connect youth to a world every bit as corporatized as the unhealthy lifestyles their parents reject, and whose role models are major marketing icons. In the end, teenagers are given a choice between two forms of consumerism: one approved by their parents and the other not. All this serves to reinforce the overall dominance of consumer culture.

One final point needs to be made about the confirmation of consumerism in teenagers: the role of fame. Recent surveys indicate that teenagers not only want to be famous but also believe they will be one day. In his book on the cult of celebrity in the USA, Jake Halpern argues that many teenagers believe that they ought to be famous simply for being themselves, that fame requires no special skills or accomplishments. Halpern describes this as the rise of 'talentless fame', and we can see examples of it on television reality shows and on thousands of self-made online videos, blogs and personal websites.[24] Disturbingly, fame and wealth have become the most desired ambitions of our youth. But none of this should be surprising because it is simply the culmination of a childhood immersed in media, particularly the Internet, and the ideas of self-invention and self-expression. What is the point of inventing or expressing one's individuality if no one notices? So, just as a great speaker wants a large audience, a self-expressing teenager craves fame.

What are the implications of the pervasive nature of consumerism in the lives of our children? Many argue that children now learn early to navigate persuasive pitches and develop capacities for critical judgements while, of course, enjoying the benefits of a multiplicity of goods. Indeed, some reckon that children's exposure to the digital world has increased their creativity, though recent research suggests the opposite is true.[25] Others believe we are experiencing the birth pangs of a new and glorious age, a positive development in human evolution that is ushering in a period of unrivalled creativity and individual freedom.[26] But such rhetoric is fundamentally quasi-religious and simply emphasizes the point that the nature of consumerism is all-embracing. Strangely, an age supposedly noteworthy for its suspicion of dominant world-views and forms of absolutism has seemingly produced the most absolute and all-encompassing world-view ever known. In short, the success and ascendancy of consumerism demands a powerful critique and challenge in order for there to be a viable alternative. Otherwise, the promise of choice that supporters of consumerism promote is undermined from the beginning.

Many critics of youth culture point to the steep rise in anxiety-related issues among teenagers – such as increasing suicide rates, antisocial behaviour problems and depression – as proof that consumerism is a destructive force in the lives of our children.[27] But while the increase is undoubtedly true and certainly correlates with the expansion of marketing and technology in our world, many researchers have argued that so far there has been little evidence showing a causal relationship between the two.[28] Much more evidence does indicate that the lifestyles of children and teenagers have resulted in new and serious health issues: the rise in the rates of obesity, hypertension and Type 2 diabetes has been particularly noted.[29] But while it does seem evident that the media-saturated world of our children has led to serious health issues, this is probably not a useful line of criticism of consumerism as a whole. The recommended solutions to these problems – sport and exercise – are just as much a part of our consumer culture as sitting on a couch in front of the television. One of the most visible symbols of consumerism is the fitness club, and new motion-sensitive game systems like the Nintendo Wii and Microsoft Connect are proving that children can have their cake and eat it too.

There are at least three serious implications of the commodification of our youth. First, teenagers are introduced to a life that is environmentally unsustainable. The amount of resources required to provide a steady flow of products – none of which remain long in fashion – is staggering, especially in comparison to the requirements of children 40 years ago or for the majority of children worldwide today. For many parents, the dependency of children on products is a major financial drain, especially as almost all types of play now require an outlay of funds. As children have been trained always to want, they do not long remain satisfied with what they own or experience and the discarding of old toys and outdated gadgets (not to mention the batteries) amounts to a great deal of waste. In short, commodified children have learned to exploit the earth to meet their desires. As we are discovering, this is an extremely dangerous mindset.

Second, our youth begin to see themselves as commodities. Having been brought up in a world in which everything seems to be branded, they develop the instinct to brand themselves. Before the advent of the second generation of Internet technology (Web 2.0), the means for self-branding were limited: individualized presentation was largely about style of clothing, particular attention-seeking activities or choice of music. But now the Internet offers a number of ways for teenagers to brand themselves: be it on MySpace and Facebook, through a constant stream of texts and tweets or videos on YouTube. The Internet gives people, and especially teenagers, the ability to present a self-image they think will attract an audience. The Web is now littered with branded, teenage personalities who have marketed themselves successfully enough to enjoy a large and loyal audience. The commodification of the self during adolescence is a vital experience within consumerism because it provides the skills for people to develop winning personalities and to sell themselves on the job market during adulthood. In all this, focus is placed more on image and presentation than on character. It also reinforces the idea that self-worth depends on the freedom to express an identity through lifestyle symbols and for that expression to be accepted by others.

Finally, our youth have been instilled with a set of values that attenuate their capacity to achieve a degree of lasting happiness. While one may point to any number of examples of this, I will highlight only two, as I believe they have important ramifications for the Church. First, our youth are encouraged to develop an elevated sense of entitlement. From the cradle, they have been bombarded with the message that they have a right not just to have their basic needs satisfied but also to have their every desire fulfilled. At one level, this means that they enter their adulthood with the belief that it is the job of others to provide them with any and all the services they desire. As a result, human agency is often presented not as the capacity to engage the world actively but to command services effectively. Second, the prevalence of entertainment from early childhood dramatically shapes their conception and perception of pleasure. Television, the Internet, console games, theme parks, popular music and concerts and sporting events have taught our youth that pleasure must be stimulating and distracting. That they engage easily and passively in most of these activities only bolsters the expectation that pleasure is easily attainable, requires little work and ought to be oriented towards the gratification of one's own desires. It also creates a dependency – an addiction, if you will – on various technological vehicles for the experience of pleasure. Many children and teenagers find time away from stimulating technology difficult to manage, as parents who have taken their kids hiking or camping well know. Youth are taught only with great difficulty to enjoy things for their own sake or to manage boredom. Entertainment crowds out delight and the fear of boredom leads to unrealistic expectations about the character of daily existence. What both have in common is an inability of our youth to manage stillness and quiet; their attention span simply cannot cope.

Once our adolescents have reached adulthood, they must find ways for the cult of consumerism to connect with their adult experiences. This is the point when they join the rest of us adults on our pilgrimage towards self-invented happiness. We have prepared them well to join in our networks and lifestyles and to connect with us on our terms and according to the language we understand. We can expect them as adults to abide by the expectations and aspirations of consumerism in most aspects of their adult life – their leisure, relationships, work and care – and at all the key experiences: companionship, parenthood and old age. But to see how all this works in more detail, we must now turn our attention to the other sacraments of consumerism.

3

The consumer rites of adulthood

Christians regularly speak of an individual's role in the Church or society in terms of a divine calling or vocation. Young men and women are often encouraged not so much to be whatever they want or to pick a satisfying career as to discern the kind of life to which God is calling them. Obviously, this is a highly subjective activity – few people have 'road to Damascus' experiences – and, thus, susceptible to wish-fulfilment. Be that as it may, a sense of vocation ideally helps define a person's life and goals within the framework of a wider society and directs it towards a greater purpose. The vocation is fulfilled within a body – namely, the Church – and derives its meaning from that context. This vocation is answered and fulfilled with the help of the sacraments. The two obvious examples of vocational sacraments are marriage and ordination: each enacts a state of life, defines what that a state is, and provides the grace whereby people may grow towards the ideal established by the sacrament. So, for example, at a wedding a couple become 'one flesh' through the exchange of vows, understand their marriage as sacramental union (as opposed to a mere legal contract), and receive grace to discover how to live in mutual submission and loving service. The other sacraments can also be understood within the context of vocations: confession provides the forgiveness and restoration necessary for sanctification, unction the healing of soul and body in times of ill-health, and, finally, the Eucharist the nourishment of soul and spirit within the body of Christ.

Just as the Church has vocations that are defined and sustained by the sacraments, so too does consumerism. In his book *Consuming Life*, the sociologist Zygmunt Bauman notes:

> As soon as they learn to read, or perhaps well before, children's 'shop dependence' sets in . . . In a society of consumers, *everyone* needs to be, ought to be, must be a consumer-by-vocation

(that is, view and treat consumption as a vocation); in that society, consumption-seen-and-treated-as-vocation is one universal human right *and* universal duty that knows of no exception.[1]

According to Bauman, consumerism-as-vocation arises because consumer society demands that individuals develop 'consumer skills and patterns of actions' to obtain the products and services required for their chosen lifestyle and sense of well-being – and to be seen to be doing so successfully.[2] Ultimately, individuals are successful only by transforming themselves into commodities: they must become 'saleable' by 'obtaining the qualities for which there is already a market demand, or recycling the qualities already possessed into commodities for which demand can go on to be created'.[3] Every aspect of humanity is objectified as resources for self-development: bodies are to be improved (through diet, fitness or cosmetics), minds made useful (through job skills, self-help guides and religion), and personalities made attractive (through therapy and lifestyle choices).

Consumerism-as-vocation is conducted through a series of acts and experiences in life that can be broken down along lines similar to the sacramental rites of adulthood: marriage, confession, healing, priesthood and the Eucharist. Each act or experience either helps to define how consumerism-as-vocation is expressed and realized or provides the ideal towards which it strives. Within the quasi-sacramental life of consumerism, individuals construct identities through their lifestyles and discover the means for pursuing the promise of happiness and self-fulfilment. In other words, consumerism-as-vocation is conducted within the quasi-sacramental environment of consumer culture: people use goods and services (1) to invent themselves within relationships, (2) to provide themselves with means for doing so through confession and healing (striving for 'authenticity' and therapeutic wholeness), (3) to avail themselves of the services of consumerism's priesthood (experts, managers and celebrities), and (4) to exist as a consumer society by feeding off the very system of which they are part in a kind of eucharistic parody.

Consumerism and relationships: sex and partnership

At one level, the emphasis consumer culture places on relationships, particularly romantic ones, is ironic: it is not particularly obvious why one self-actualizing person would want to enter into a relationship with another. After all, that very relationship places unavoidable constraints on a person's journey towards an authentic identity and personal happiness. For example, because I elected to marry my wife there are certain choices now excluded from me: I cannot enter into sexual relationships with others, easily enjoy a lifestyle that places her in an intolerable position, or spend my time and money as I choose. Seen in this light, the free love popularly attributed to bohemians is the natural outcome of consumerism because it allows for gratification of biological urges without any unpleasant limits placed on individual choice and expression. Yet, strangely, most people find themselves either unable or unwilling to pursue such a lifestyle throughout their life. Why is this?

There are two main reasons why even in an age of self-invention and hyper-individualism people feel drawn to enter into meaningful relationships with one another. The more obvious answer is that as *Homo sapiens* we are biologically predisposed towards developing stable sexual relationships, though not necessarily monogamous ones. Whatever their personal beliefs, therefore, most people feel an inescapable urge to form sexual bonds of attachment that are dependable. Additionally, marketing and business have employed sexual relationships to promote products, attractive lifestyles and notions of happiness. One of the most effective ways to attract attention is to advertise one's sexual availability through style and activities. Also, we have been repeatedly offered a presentation of a kind of faithful cohabitation that supposedly brings with it all sorts of psychological and health benefits: less chance of sexually transmitted diseases, emotional support, increased standard of living, dependable sexual intimacy. Countless books promote committed sexual relationships in precisely these terms, collecting an impressive array of research to support their claims about the many personal benefits of monogamous cohabitation. As a result, we now speak of 'healthy relationships' and have a very definite idea of what that means. Innumerable popular songs, films and shows help to create a powerful myth about relationships that not only is a profitable industry in itself but also becomes for us the ideal of romantic engagements; we come to judge our own relationships by that market-generated ideal.

The popularized ideal of romantic relationships is incredibly important to consumers because we conduct our lives in a world saturated with sex, be it images in advertising, presentations in our films and shows, explicit language in our popular songs, or in our fashion and lifestyles. From its inception, the self-actualization movement viewed sexual liberation as an integral part of the process of achieving an authentic identity and personal happiness. Indeed, most people find the idea of happiness apart from complete sexual fulfilment difficult to imagine, even though both research and anecdotal evidence suggest that few achieve the lasting fulfilment that the myth promises. So, just as we are digesting a fabricated ideal of committed relationships, we are being bombarded with sexualized images that shape our desires, expectations and the way we understand our own sexuality. All of this suits our consumer culture well because nothing sells like sex.

Since our ideal of relationships is advertised in terms of personal benefits and human flourishing, it consequently becomes self-oriented. Marriage and partnerships are rarely defended in terms of their public good as in most non-consumer societies. So, for example, in the Book of Common Prayer, it (or rather Matrimony) is described as an 'honourable estate' or a condition of life within society that is ordained for the procreation of children, continence and 'mutual society'. To be a husband or wife, therefore, is to have a particular role within society, to enjoy certain privileges (sex and companionship) and to undertake certain obligations (mutual support and producing children). One entered into marriage hopefully out of love but more often (at least among the middle and upper classes) to solidify relations between families and to function visibly as a societal glue. Not until relatively recent times has marriage been understood to be the natural result of romantic love. Indeed, this remains a foreign concept in much of the world.

None of this is to suggest that the traditional understanding of marriage is preferable but only to indicate how attitudes have changed. Except in some decidedly conservative advice books or in the public debate about gay marriages, one will rarely encounter a presentation of marriage as primarily a public good or a social act. Marriage and its reasons are by and large private, to be undertaken and understood by the couple alone. In fact, the mere suggestion that marriage has a public role for the good of society is found by many to be abhorrent. Since committed sexual relationships now lack an obvious public role, they are typically described in terms of how they can

41

benefit the individuals who enter into them. Consequently, relationships that have become 'toxic' to one's own well-being are deemed 'unhealthy' and best ended.

Despite the promotion of relationships within a consumer society, the ideal of individual self-expression and invention remains dominant. This obviously creates a dilemma: how both to be committed to someone else and remain as free as possible to pursue personal fulfilment and happiness. The solution arose during the 1980s and 1990s out of an altogether different problem: how inclusively to describe both married and unmarried couples. Drawing predictably from the commercial world, the acceptable term for committed relationship has come to be termed 'partnership'. In business, a partnership is an agreement between two independent entities to enter into a contractual relationship for mutual profit. Within the partnership, each entity retains the freedom to look to its own best interests (in so far as they do not harm the other). But the impetus for entering into the partnership is the recognition by both parties that some of those interests are best served by working together. And this is how we have come popularly to conceive of committed sexual relationships. Within such partnerships it is both permissible and advisable for each partner to remain as independent as possible, to advocate for his or her own rights (depicted as needs), but also to support the partnership itself for the benefit of each other and their children.[4] Like a commercial partnership, however, either partner may end the relationship if it no longer serves his or her best interests. Indeed, if either member believes the partnership no longer allows him or her to enjoy life properly, then the expectation is that separation will soon follow; hence one of the salient features of consumer culture is a high rate of divorce and separation. Ultimately what is most important to individuals is that they always have the freedom to progress towards whatever identity or lifestyle they desire.

Finally, one cannot discuss relationships within consumer culture without drawing attention to how the act of union itself – the wedding – has become almost entirely commodified. It is now the apotheosis of consumerism: the essential hen and stag nights, the exhibition of products and services at wedding shows and in bridal magazines, the outpouring of money on image and display, and the extravagant receptions afterwards. Together these focus attention on the event itself and seek to align the experience with an ideal portrayed through the media. According to one survey, the average wedding and reception now costs over £15,000 (double that of ten years ago), of which the legal fees are only the smallest fraction.[5] And couples typically do not feel compelled to spend such vast sums but are eager to do so because it places the wedding experience within the familiar territory established through the media. In other words, the reality is what has been presented in films and in magazines while the wedding event only aspires to such reality through lavish expense. Indeed, for a day, the couple can mimic the lifestyle of the rich and famous without the risk of disapproval.

The confession of a consumer: publicity

Some may argue that consumerism has no equivalent to the Church's sacrament of confession and reconciliation since consumers have little conception of sin. But a certain kind of confession permeates our society and functions as one of the guiding principles for how people ought to conduct their lives: publicity, understood as both the presentation of private life in the media and the belief that personal authenticity requires a degree of self-advertising normally styled as honesty. As with the sacrament of confession, it exposes what is otherwise hidden and is a means of transformation. By advertising private lives or an 'authentic' identity for public consumption, people can attract an audience that validates their lifestyle and identity.

Publicity does not require misconduct but only the attention, however briefly, of others. In his book *Common Objects of Love*, the moral theologian Oliver O'Donovan describes the first kind of publicity this way:

> publicity is a kind of universal gaze. But unlike fame, it selects its subjects with apparent arbitrariness, irrespective of what they have achieved, and unlike glory, it selects them without reference to the public institutions in which they shine. The visibility given by publicity is neither the radiance of accomplishment nor the floodlighting of major social institutions. It is a roaming spotlight, catching people unpredictably in its beam. It does not accrue to projects, planning, virtues of performance, teamwork, durable results, or anything of merit. It is interested only in those moments over which its subjects have little or no control:

their spontaneous reactions or their embattled struggles. Publicity
is attracted not by achievement, but by pathos.[6]

He goes on to argue that the purpose of publicity is to 'evoke' recognition from the general public in order to create interest and to generate common representations. These common images – Princess Diana's funeral is a prime example – provide a shared cultural currency within the imagination of consumer society by which people can show themselves to be socially competent; knowing the minute details of 'publicity events' carries a degree of social cachet that demonstrates a person's cultural sophistication.

O'Donovan's interest is in publicity in general and in the interplay between news, advertising and entertainment (which he argues are becoming almost indistinguishable). My interest, however, is in a particular form of publicity: the 'tell-all' stories that litter the tabloids, television programming, the Internet and, increasingly, 'hard news' outlets. Stories about celebrities, sports stars and politicians' private lives, and especially examples of misconduct, not only sell media products but also serve as a constant narrative within consumer society. The effect of these is enhanced by the multiplicity of programmes in which both celebrities and ordinary folk reveal aspects of their private lives in front of a live audience or the camera. In each of these examples, confession itself becomes a kind of entertainment, subsumed like everything else within the advertising machinery that propels consumerism. Tabloids are notorious examples of this, adorning their covers with private misdeeds in order to boost sales and attract more advertising. Such is the fever pitch of reporting on every detail of the private lives and peccadillos of the famous that we become suspicious of those who try to protect their own privacy. The famous are, therefore, presented with a stark choice: to be 'vulnerable' and honest enough to air their foibles for mass consumption or face an army of tabloid investigators who will efficiently ferret out the truth; in other words, confess or face the inquisition.

The notion of honesty connects the first kind of publicity with the belief that self-advertising is a necessary part of being authentic. Having been fed a lavish diet of advertising from the cradle, we come to think of honesty primarily in terms of advertising, of being true to oneself within the gaze of the other. There is, of course, much in philosophy and devotional literature about the importance of being honest to oneself and confronting both the good and the evil that lie within. Regular self-examination was once encouraged among all Christians. But such honesty was inherently private: an inner journey into the depths of the soul under a divine gaze conceived in terms of virtue and vice. Neoplatonists sought to be true to themselves in order to free the soul from corporeal bondage, and Christians to live according to God's will. Whether or not one's neighbour acknowledged this honesty was either secondary or merely a consequence of the reordering of one's moral actions. This is why the sacrament of confession is conducted in private: the restriction of a confessor from speaking about the confession allows for moral guidance without necessarily publicizing the interior journey towards self-knowledge. Fundamentally, honesty was understood to be about according oneself to a higher truth and seeking to see oneself – failings, strengths, behaviour and ends – from the vantage point of that higher truth.

In consumer culture, honesty is essentially about advertising one's perceived true self and convincing others to accept that publicized self. Only the acceptance of one's expressed inner self by others makes the whole endeavour meaningful. 'Being honest about yourself', therefore, is not so much about moral self-knowledge as about behaving in a way that advertises to others who you think you are or need to be in order to flourish. All the books advising people how to be honest suggest the same thing: one has to learn to resist expectations, to be free of obligations ('oughts'), and to learn how to express one's authentic self, invariably described in incredibly attractive terms. Assumed in all these books is that apart from societal expectations and influence, the self is inherently and thoroughly good; thus, as with confession, self-honesty is about divesting oneself of corruption (now understood as 'toxic' external influences) and embracing a new, 'authentic' life.[7] But this new life only has meaning if expressed openly to others, which may necessitate a reordering of relationships depending on how well others accept this new presentation. Ultimately, personal publicity seeks to reverse the flow of power: instead of individuals subjecting themselves to the demands of others, they demand that others accept their honest presentation of their own authentic self.

As we discussed in Chapter 1, this form of personal publicity creates all sorts of avenues for sales and marketing. Typically, people advertise their authentic selves through products – clothes, diets, books, music

and social activities – which provide the individual with the exhilarating sense of freedom that comes through self-expression. Indeed,
these avenues remain open because, as we have seen, it is impossible
for people ever to discover their authentic selves. Honesty and self-
invention become a way of life, demanding the constant advertising
of one's own honest self and a profound willingness on the part of
others to adapt to those changing presentations. But this is not necessarily as totally narcissistic as some critics have suggested.[8] Honesty
through personal publicity occurs not because people deliberately
want to be the centre of attention (though this may be true) but
because self-marketing is a natural form of communication in a world
saturated with advertising; our reinvention only becomes authentic
when others recognize it. We want people to applaud our honestly
presented self just as they do the introduction of a newly upgraded
product. Ultimately, authenticity through advertised honesty arises
among people who have been taught to see themselves as products;
it is surely telling that books about authenticity often tend to be about
either human psychology or the marketing of products.

The healing of consumers: the rise of a therapeutic culture

Achieving an ever-escaping authentic identity can be a lonely vocation. Scholars have often noted that within consumerist culture,
communities break down and roots break, resulting in free-floating
notions of self that are cut adrift from any communal or social identity. People often do not enjoy what they have but yearn to purchase
whatever they currently lack: no sooner do we have a new laptop,
mobile, car or television than a newer and better one appears on the
market. And we are constantly bombarded with the message that life
could be much better than it is. As a result, our sense of self is desta-
bilized and fractured; the person we think we are or who we want to
be changes regularly as different ideals and lifestyles present themselves to us like wares in a supermarket. All of this can be so wearing
on the consumer vocation that people crumble under the weight of
anxiety and turn to any number of other destructive activities to taste
the happiness they have so long been promised.

Nearly 50 years ago, the noted sociologist Philip Rieff observed that
with the loss of both a sense of the transcendent and a commitment

to communal values, individual lives became centred on a personal sense of well-being.[9] Much of this development arose directly from the rootlessness caused by the rapid industrialization of European society during the nineteenth century as millions of people became dislocated from traditional sources of identity.[10] Having been driven out of their small agrarian villages, people found themselves thrust into a new life of anonymity in urban environments, often amid horrendous living conditions. At the same time, traditional forms of Christianity began to erode and with them established beliefs about transcendent virtues and sanctions. People felt increasingly cut off from the world in which they lived and the God they worshipped, and therefore started to seek out alternative ways of achieving a sense of well-being. This was the age in which 'spiritual' lifestyles (such as the various forms of theosophy), initial developments in psychiatric practice, and popularized forms of healthy living (such as the efforts of the Kellogg brothers) all emerged.

Rieff argues that one of the main reasons for the rise of therapeutic culture was the collapse of social identities within well-defined communities. Before the nineteenth century, therapy was largely religious in nature and engaged in the reintegration of individuals into their community through the development and refinement of character.[11] In a sense, this was the purpose of the priestly cure of souls. But with the collapse of those communities, therapy became personal and redirected from questions of character to those of personality. Vincent Miller writes:

> In a social world reconfigured in terms of market competition, individuals were forced to market themselves by cultivating 'winning' personality traits as well as appearance, hygiene, and health. A host of cultural elites – physicians, psychologists, and Christian ministers – offered an ideology of the self to assist people in accomplishing these tasks. These therapeutic programs portrayed security, vitality, and harmony as personal concerns and responsibilities that could be achieved without social change.[12]

By the late twentieth century, one of the main ways people maintained a sense of well-being and a 'winning' personality was through recourse to psychiatric drugs. Indeed, the spectacular rise in the purveyance of pharmaceuticals during the 1990s epitomizes both the role of corporations and advertising in the development of personal identities and the importance of appearance over reality; the effects of the drugs as advertised conform to a cultural norm (a happy, contented person) and too often the drugs are taken to mask deep-seated and often unexamined issues.

The quote from Vincent Miller indicates that the presumption of therapeutic culture is that the primary threats to well-being are to be found less in the ordering of society than in inner problems that need to be diagnosed and treated.[13] As we saw in Chapter 1, some criticize the self-actualization movement for pacifying social discontent. If the reason for my sense of unhappiness has to do with my needing the tools and space to express my true, inner self, then I am less likely to be concerned about the social conditions in which I live. My only expectation will be that society provides sufficient freedom of choice for me to express myself in whatever way I believe to be most authentic and honest. This partly explains why contemporary debates tend to be more about matters of choice and identity (questions of equality and tolerance) than about the structure of contemporary society itself. In other words, we carry on those debates within a consumer culture without calling that culture into question. What worries us is not the common good but free access to the means of achieving well-being; the assumption is that the common good arises through individuals achieving their authentic identities and sense of well-being.

An overly myopic focus on personal well-being can lead to a mis-interpretation of social ills; someone's sense that the world is somehow wrong may have something to do either with that person's psychology or with the fact that there is something wrong with the world. But within a therapeutic culture, that individual is likely to be diagnosed with a number of different psychiatric disorders (from mild depression to psychosis), undergo therapy and be prescribed medication to help him or her cope; the question as to whether there may be good societal reasons why that person feels isolated and depressed will probably never be investigated or even asked. Instead, therapeutic efforts will be devoted to enabling the person to resume a fulfilling and productive journey towards achieving a satisfying and expressed identity. In short, the therapist seeks to restore clients to their vocation as consumers.

This last statement may seem unfair to the practice of therapy. On one level, therapy plays a crucial role in helping people confront and cope with very real emotional disorders. But therapy can also have a normative effect, assuming as typical a manner of living that is decidedly suburban and Western in character, not least because this is the culture in which therapists themselves often live. Indeed, the pervasive presentations of psychic wholeness become another one of those ideals towards which consumers strive (and expect to reach) through the purchase of services (therapy) and products (drugs). So, for example, someone who is depressed and struggles with a persistent sense of loneliness or feels adrift is treated as someone in need of therapy even though, as we have seen, these are typical effects of consumerism. Ultimately, the seemingly happy consumer provides the psychiatric model to which everyone ought to conform or undergo treatment. This should not be surprising given the roots of consumer culture within psychological analysis.

Consumerism's priesthood: managers, experts and celebrities

Catholicism conceives of priestly authority in three different forms: episcopal, pastoral and ideological. Episcopal authority directs the Church in its many functions and binds Christians together through dioceses and provinces. Pastoral authority impacts on personal lives either through pastoral care, preaching or the provision of sacramental rites. Alongside these two forms of authority, and often functioning independently, is the ideological authority represented by the saints, whose lives model an ideal to which the faithful are devoted and towards which they may strive. The authority of the bishop, priest and saint depends on their being either guardians of an essential but complex knowledge (the means of salvation) or embodiments of cultural ideals (i.e. the saints). These three 'priestly' roles find their equivalent in consumer society in the characters of the manager, the expert and the celebrity.[14] The manager directs and organizes people within bureaucratic systems, the expert (therapist, physician, hygienist, investment advisor, etc.) provides knowledge for individuals within a highly complex society, and the celebrity embodies and celebrates the underlying ideology of consumerism. Furthermore, just as a priest or a bishop might also become a saint, so may managers and experts become celebrities, as in the case (on the one hand) of Mark Zuckerberg, Richard Branson, Steve Jobs and (on the other) of a whole host of lifestyle, health and fashion gurus. As with the medieval priesthood, the authority of managers, experts and celebrities relies on the perception that they possess knowledge within a system that is too complex for individuals to decipher for themselves.

A defining feature of late modernity is the managerial system under which companies, governments, universities, schools and even the Church operate. Successful organizations make efficient use of their resources, reduce the time needed to produce their products or services, standardize what is offered over time and in all locations, and control the decisions of their customers and workers.[15] Chief among these resources are the workers themselves. In recent decades, the same trends that introduced lifestyle marketing have radically transformed the old Fordist managerialism into what is called human resources management (HRM), which employs psychological techniques to align human resources with current business strategy, facilitate the re-engineering of organizational processes, listen and respond to employees to encourage commitment and competency, and ensure capacity for future change.[16] Just as primary resources are developed into secondary ones (as in, for example, the production of aluminium), so too are human resources developed into more efficient and more highly committed workers through 'personal development'. So, now employees expect both their work and personality to be evaluated by their managers, effectively eliding the distinction between public and private persona and enabling the manipulation of individual identities; indeed, personal development schemes shape how people perceive well-being.[17] Not surprisingly, this transformation is accomplished using many of the same psychological techniques developed in the marketing world.

Human resources management has now been exported into many different areas of society: education, health, social services, finances and the Church.[18] Increasingly, we live in a 'HRM constructed world' that conforms to the generic practices of HRM: 'benchmarking, thresholds, quality circle notions of standards and evaluation, arbitrary performance indicators, single scale job evaluation, selective privatization and short-term contracts, and the gradual displacement of "education" by "training" and "skills acquisition" at all levels'.[19] Managerialism, therefore, functions as the engine of consumer culture, efficiently managing the necessary resources (human or otherwise) to produce the goods and services necessary to meet public consumption. As a result, efficiency and happiness become inextricably intertwined. And within that world, the manager functions like a bishop, both directing the various structures of consumer culture and representing power and leadership for others to mimic through guidebooks, residential courses and conferences.

Experts thrive within a consumer culture because that culture contains an incredibly complex array of complicated systems that no single person can master. Thus, we have experts to help with finance, advise on nutrition and health, help achieve psychic well-being, explain new technologies and techniques, and decipher the law and world events. And because modern culture is so complicated, people cannot really do without them: we depend on their services just as much as the laity depended on priestly care during the Middle Ages. And like them people generally are happy to pay a premium in order to obtain their assurance of success, be it good health, financial security, fashion sense or sports acumen.

In his analysis of 'expert systems', Anthony Giddens makes two important and seemingly contradictory points.[20] First, whereas social relations were formerly conducted primarily through face-to-face encounters within a particular locale, now they are typically conducted with strangers whose authority relies on the 'disembedded' system in which they operate. Second, since experts are strangers, those who avail themselves of their knowledge and skills must display a level of trust. We cannot trust the people themselves as they are strangers, so instead we come to trust the 'expert systems' in which they function. Credentials make this phenomenon possible: proof of expertise gives people the assurance that the provider has been 'authorized' by the 'expert system' to provide the desired service. As a result, experts are less individuals than access points to expert systems. In other words, we go to a therapist, a doctor or an invest-ment advisor to obtain the services of the system they represent (psychiatry, medical care, finance) rather than to engage in a face-to-face relationship with the man or woman who happens to fill that role. Giddens argues that this leads to an emphasis on demeanour within expert systems – 'the grave deliberations of the judge, the sombre professionalism of the doctor, or the stereotyped cheerfulness of the cabin crew' – in order to reassure people that the 'access points' and the expert system are genuine.[21] As a result, people routinely allow themselves to be deeply influenced by abstract, 'faceless' sys-tems about which they know little. Furthermore, these faceless and disembedded systems provide the means and tools for people to pursue happiness and self-invention. This leads to an ironic situation in which people seek to invent their personalities free from external influences by abiding by the expertise of impersonal systems.

Finally, we come to the saints of consumerism: celebrities. Much has been written about the advent and promotion of celebrity culture in high modernity and so there is no need here to rehearse the many criticisms made about the growing 'obsession' with celebrities.[22] One of the more useful and dispassionate analyses of celebrity culture is Graeme Turner's *Understanding Celebrity*. In his section on the social role of celebrities, he draws upon the work of other sociologists to suggest that the 'para-social' relationships individuals form with celebrities and the gossip they share about them help people to question and develop cultural identities and notions of individualism. By way of explanation, he cites Richard Dyer who argues that celebrities function as 'signs' embedded with cultural meaning that audiences read like texts that are 'ideologically saturated and discursively constructed'.[23] The deep emotional response to Diana's death and funeral and the cultural experience of those events is an example of this process.

In his book *Celebrity*, Chris Rojek argues that this 'para-social' function of celebrities is not unlike the role of shamans within traditional cultures.[24] He notes:

Celebrities offer peculiarly powerful affirmations of belonging, recognition and meaning in the midst of the lives of their audiences, lives that may otherwise be poignantly experienced as under-performing, anti-climactic or sub-clinically depressing. A peculiar tension in celebrity culture is that the physical and social remoteness of the celebrity is compensated for by the glut of mass-media information, including fanzines, press stories, TV documentaries, newsletters and biographies, which personalize the celebrity, turning a distant figure from a stranger into a significant other. The tension has inescapable parallels with religious worship, and these are reinforced by the attribution by fans of magical or extraordinary powers to the celebrity. Celebrities are thought to possess God-like qualities by some fans, while others – experiencing the power of the celebrity to arouse deep emotions – recognize the spirit of the shaman.[25]

Rojek uses other characteristic ways people relate to and interact with celebrities (such as collecting autographs and memorabilia, making pilgrimages to their places of death, and even stalking) to argue that celebrity culture fills the vacuum of 'organizing recognition and belonging' left by the retreat of institutional religion from daily life.[26] People now adore celebrities, collect their memorabilia as relics, and celebrate the ideal they represent in much the same way people once did with saints. If Chaucer were writing today, the pilgrims would make their way to Graceland rather than to Canterbury.

Celebrities draw part of their power from the way they are able to represent so many ideals of consumerism: they constantly reinvent their images, are seen to be pursuing successfully their own self-actualized identity, publicize every detail of their lives, and present themselves as having achieved happiness. They epitomize the ends towards which consumerism compels people and embody the ideals that almost everyone has absorbed from the cradle. The hagiography of celebrities is so powerful that most people are not in the slightest bothered or even interested in all the lives wrecked and ruined in the pursuit of a celebrity lifestyle. Thanks also to their unremitting presence through various media, they also do not seem nearly as distant as saints; they are a visible cloud of witnesses that surround consumers – in them person and icon are entirely united so that relating to the image and to the person are completely interchangeable.

The shared meal of consumers: mass consumption

In this survey of consumerism through the lens of the sacraments, I have deliberately left the Eucharist to the end because it encompasses the other rites of consumerism. Within Catholicism, the Eucharist is the sacrament that undergirds the whole Christian life. Baptism and confirmation point to it, the ordained ministry enables it, marriage ideally embodies it, and reconciliation and unction depend on it. The reason for this is that the Eucharist is none other than the body of Christ himself, however that mystery is understood. To partake of the Eucharist is to be united intimately with Christ and to be drawn into and nourished by Divine Love. But as Augustine of Hippo recognized long ago, Christians do not stand apart from the Eucharist (like people do from regular food) but are themselves members of the body of Christ. So, in what is arguably the central mystery of Christian life, the body of Christ is nourished by the body of Christ. As Augustine explains, 'there you are on the table, and there you are in the cup. You are this together with us; we all take this together, all drink together, because we all live together.'[27]

In much the same way, mass consumption is the central sacrament of consumerism that undergirds everything else; it is by consuming goods and services, each other, and even the self, that people sustain consumerism. Everything must be packaged and repackaged as a commodity or else be discarded as waste (which, in a perverse parody of the feeding of the five thousand, is gathered up and consumed either as recycled goods or as an increasingly profitable business of waste management). Consumption is, therefore, what makes sense of everything else: unless people and things do something for us, we ignore or discard them. From this relentless and pervasive consumption arises the whole system of consumerism. In this way, mass consumption is reflexive – consumerism can only continue to exist by feeding upon itself and all its constituent parts. This can be seen clearly in terms of economic policies, especially during recessions when governments plead for people to go shopping and spend their money rather than build up savings. In such cases, consumption becomes a moral good, providing the economic means for the government to continue to provide all the public services that people demand. The self-consumption of consumerism is just as present in individual lives, as we have now seen. People's identities have been so influenced and wrapped up in consumption that it is only by continuing to consume that those identities can be sustained. In his book on the relationship between consumerism and culture, the anthropologist Grant David McCracken argues:

> Without consumer goods, modern, developed societies would lose key instruments for the reproduction, representation, and manipulation of their culture. The worlds of design, product development, advertising, and fashion are themselves important authors of our cultural universe. They work constantly to shape, transform, and vivify our universe. Without them the modern world would almost certainly come undone. The meaning of consumer goods and the meaning creation accomplished by consumer processes are important parts of the scaffolding of

our present realities. Without consumer goods, certain acts of self-definition and collective definition in this world would be impossible.[28]

Meaning and identity become inextricably bound up in the act of consumption. As we have seen, this consumption can take many different forms and be conducted in many different ways, but in every case it serves to bolster consumerism's hold over people. Just as the Eucharist within the Catholic tradition is believed to provide the nourishment for life and the grace to fulfil the Christian vocation, so too does each and every act of consumption reinforce our vocation as consumers and further shape and limit how we perceive ourselves and the world in which we live. To put this boldly, whenever we are presented with an advert, go shopping, seek out psychic well-being, sit in front of the television, surf the Internet or upgrade our mobile, consumerism says to us, 'This is my body' and 'This is my blood'. We respond by partaking of the fruits of consumerism and go away satisfied, if only fleetingly, further confirmed that this life and this vocation are our highest calling.

4

A Church for consumer tribes

The rapidity with which consumer culture arose and dominated Western society was matched only by the collapse of the Church as a meaningful influence (with the notable exception of the USA) in most people's lives. Contrary to popular opinion, however, mass secularization did not begin with the Enlightenment or even with the industrialization and urbanization of European society. In fact, the nineteenth century was by and large a strongly religious age. Instead, widespread secularization is really coterminous with the rise of mass consumption and consumerism. In other words, secularization is a feature not of a post-Enlightenment society but of a consumer one. For the majority of people in Europe, to be a conspicuous consumer means not to be an active member of the Church.

Among the best studies of religion in the age of consumerism are Callum Brown's *The Death of Christian Britain* and Grace Davie's equally important work, especially her *Religion in Britain since 1945*. Brown's thesis is that mass secularization did not really begin until around 1958, after which it swept away most forms of popular religious observance within little more than a decade. He proposes that a key reason for this was the 'simultaneous de-pietisation of femininity and the defeminisation of piety' during the 1960s and 1970s, which resulted in a mass exodus of women and their children from regular religious participation.[1] Davie, for her part, argues that a decline in church attendance is not the same as a decline in religious belief. Drawing upon the work of the sociologist David Martin, she prefers the idea of 'belief without belonging' to describe the rise of a form of vicarious Christianity in which a small minority observe their faith and maintain churches on behalf of the majority. Both works demonstrate that the decline of the Church in Western society is due less to secularization than to the rise of hyper-consumerism; more to the point, only after the emergence of corporate mass marketing did churches lose their central place in Western society.

Faced with steep decline and a swiftly changing society, the Church has adapted to consumerism both deliberately through policy decisions and unintentionally as a result of the transformation of Christians into conspicuous consumers. By and large, this commodi-fication of Christianity can be seen in everything from the increas-ingly profitable contemporary Christian music industry to the many forms of devotional practice that are directed towards niche markets (such as Celtic spirituality) and the branding of church initiatives (such as the Alpha course and fresh expressions of church). Similarly, church assemblies have often debated consumer issues (questions about the latitude of choice, identity, managerial policies) without clearly recognizing that fact or articulating a distinctly Christian way of addressing them. Even more profoundly, the Church has allowed itself by varying degrees to become a niche lifestyle within con-sumer culture. A critical characteristic of any religion for many peo-ple today is that it affirms or expresses their chosen lifestyle. People have long 'shopped' for their church of choice in the USA and are increasingly doing so in the UK. As a result, churches are pressured to conform to consumer demands, often resulting in congregational identities that reflect the sociopolitical divisions of wider society. Moreover, the impact of consumer culture on evangelism, worship and the Church's polity (and their relationship with one another) has resulted in a Christian identity that often reflects the shape and expectations of that culture in ways that are problematic. This last point becomes clear in the 2004 report *Mission-shaped Church* and the initiative Fresh Expressions,[2] neither of which account sufficiently for the role of corporate marketing in our culture and, therefore, unintentionally absorb much of its rhetoric and concerns.

The ebbing of British Christianity

Before we can truly appreciate Callum Brown's and Grace Davie's arguments regarding the decline of the Church in Britain, we should briefly look at the historical relationship between Christianity and wider European culture during the long period when the Church and society were identified with each other.[3] Within European civilization, to be a member of society was to be a member of the

Church; even after the Reformation, most people were members of the national or Established Church. Laws generally reflected Christian beliefs, education inculcated scriptural knowledge, public officials openly professed their faith, and literature and the arts typically expressed Christian themes. Although all of this had been eroded by the dawn of the twentieth century, the general assumption remained that Western society was Christian and that, therefore, no clear distinction ought to be made between Christian and national mores.

This identification of the Church with wider society encouraged a lively debate during the nineteenth and twentieth centuries as Western culture (particularly its intellectual elements) began to distance itself from Christian doctrines. The Church struggled to discern how much modernity could be accommodated without fundamentally compromising the faith. In England, the publication of *Essays and Reviews* and *Soundings*[4] represented significant, if controversial, attempts to retain a close link between the Church and a society that seemed increasingly to embrace science and rationalism. As radical as *Soundings* supposedly was, in reality its authors were attempting to bridge the widening gap between church teachings and societal beliefs, to reconstruct a comfortable identification of the Church with Western society. The authors assumed that the revolutionary changes introduced by the Enlightenment were permanent and that society was inevitably progressing towards greater scientific enlightenment. In their view, therefore, the Church had to adapt or else be left behind, an assumption that continues to undergird many of the proposals for restructuring the Church and reinterpreting its doctrine and practice.

The conformity of Christianity to modernity provides a cautionary tale about a too easy identification of the Church with societal trends. During the eighteenth and nineteenth centuries, Christians were among the most vocal proponents of industrialization and empire-building. Faithful churchgoers could engage in chattel slavery, run brutal mills and pits, and champion even the most brazen land grabs in Africa and Asia. A particularly illuminating chapter is the eugenics movement of the early twentieth century that drew some of the most 'enlightened' minds of the Church to advocate from the pulpit strict marriage regulations and enforced sterilization.[5] They adapted to their post-millennial theology the popular 'social Darwinist' premise that science ought to be used to 'improve' the species in order to secure the survival of humanity and to inaugurate an industrial utopia. In point of fact, the new truths of modernity turned out to be not all that long-lived; during the 1960s and 1970s a cultural sea-change swept away much of the established rationalism of modernity and ushered in a postmodern age. This ought at the very least to have taught the Church that societal changes are not as enduring as often assumed. Instead, the Church was swept up in or, indeed, swept away by the rise of consumerism. In desperation, the Church began trying to provide space for the new lifestyles in order to remain both relevant and welcoming to all sectors of consumer society. This process of decline and adaption are what Brown and Davie chart in their respective books.

Callum Brown begins by pointing out that sociologists of religion have not properly accounted for the astonishing vigour of English Christianity during the 1940s and 1950s, when the UK experienced the greatest church growth in almost 100 years.[6] He argues that this alone casts doubt on the assumption that Britain's secularization was a relentless movement that began well before the present age. Brown suggests, however, that the vigour of the Church during the post-war period was due, at least in part, to 'the state's promotion of "pro-natalism", of women's place being in the home where the nation needed an invigorated birth rate to overcome labour shortage'.[7] One of the primary means of promoting this image was through magazines, which presented for female consumption an ideal of a happy wife and mother.[8] The idealization of the traditional values of home, family and piety led directly to an increase in church attendance, Sunday school enrolment and confirmations.

According to Brown, the growth and strength of churches in the UK was entirely dependent on female piety. In the 1960s, however, the ending of excessive moral censorship, the termination of the Lord Chamberlain's control over the theatre, legalization of abortion and homosexual activity, granting of easier divorce, the women's liberation movement, and the emergence of the student-led youth culture served as catalysts for the 'de-pietisation' of women.[9] Together, these swept away earlier stereotypes and ushered in new feminine ideals over which the Church had little or no say. Again, magazines were key to promoting new feminine identities; Brown surveys both those magazines that did not adapt and so quickly failed (such as *Housewife*) and those that connected with and promoted the new ideals (such as *Boyfriend, Jackie* and *Everywoman*).[10] As women embraced the modern image, they no longer valued the traditional role of being the religious heart of society. Brown writes:

> The loss of domestic ideology to youth culture from *c.* 1958 meant that piety 'lost' its discursive home with femininity ... The distinctive growth in the 1950s of women's dual role in home and work was a major contributing factor, creating a new stress about which model defined a woman's 'duty', upsetting the salience of evangelical protocols, and rendering women part of the same religious 'problem' as men. The reconstruction of female identity within work, sexual relations and new recreational opportunities from the late 1960s, put not just feminism but female identity in collision with the Christian construction of femininity.[11]

The subsequent haemorrhaging of the Church was astonishing. The British began to reject all regular forms of religious practice, leading to precipitous declines in attendance, baptisms, weddings and Sunday school participation.[12] The initial abandonment of religious observance by formerly practising Christians meant that subsequent generations were 'raised in a domestic routine largely free from the intrusions of organised religion'.[13]

Grace Davie offers a slightly less desperate account of this period by examining the discrepancy between the precipitous decline in religious observance and the much more modest decline in actual religious belief. Davie explains this inconsistency by arguing that we now live in a culture of 'believing without belonging', a phrase used by others to describe a common and largely 'privatized' religion that is only nominally Christian.[14] In Davie's view, this 'vicarious religion' rather than secularism is the best description of the contemporary religious scene. Religion is now 'performed by an active minority but on behalf of a much larger number, who (implicitly at least) not only understand, but quite clearly approve of what the minority are doing'.[15] She offers as evidence of this the adverse reaction people having to pay for entry into religious buildings such as cathedrals.[16] Like Brown, Davie traces the origins of 'believing without belonging' to the 1960s and 1970s when the overall active membership of the Church of England was reduced by half.[17] But Davie links this more clearly than Brown to the rise of consumerism, arguing that 'believing without belonging' signifies a transition from a society of religious obligation to one of religious consumption: 'What until moderately recently was simply imposed (with all the negative connotations of this word), or inherited . . . becomes instead a matter of personal choice.'[18] This explains the seemingly contradictory health of cathedrals and suburban churches: both are able to offer distinctive products to diverse constituencies but often without any obligation to participate in activities beyond worship.[19]

Davie helpfully situates these developments within an overall decline in membership among political parties and trade unions and at sporting events and pubs.[20] The phrase 'believing without belonging', therefore, describes a general trend among all voluntary associations in British society. In other words, the growth of a network society has had an adverse impact on almost all concrete forms of community life in contemporary society; the Church is a prime but not unique example of this trend. People choose, rather than feel obliged, to belong to various kinds of communities (including churches); and since participation is entirely a matter of choice, people can also determine for themselves both the level and length of their commitment.[21] The primacy of choice effectively transforms all kinds of associations into a marketplace where each community is obliged to advertise and adapt itself in order to encourage involvement and survive; relevancy becomes the primary means of success.

Both Brown and Davie present a picture of modern religious life that swiftly retreated before the advance of consumerism. Although Brown does not emphasize the role of consumerism per se, it is noteworthy that he highlights magazines as important shapers of identity. The transition from magazines encouraging a 'pro-natal' femininity to those promoting a liberated one coincided with the transition from a psychiatric regulation of individual behaviour on behalf of society to a psychiatric promotion of self-expression in the face of wider society. Indeed, Brown's analysis demonstrates that the Church held its own within post-Enlightenment society until the rise of mass marketing through the media. The massive decline in regular church attendance resulted from the growing dominance of marketing as the mediator of societal mores rather than a supposed societal embrace of scientific rationalism. In short, the mass marketing of the consumer ideal of happiness through self-actualized lifestyles has led directly to the Church's decline. This has been recognized by Martyn Percy, who states:

Strictly speaking, then, the threat posed by consumerism to Christianity is not the material versus the spiritual. It is, rather, a competition between systems of meaning and identification. In this regard, we can suggest that advertising has a teleological and utopian dimension to it: it suggests a new order that is to come. In effect, it offers a promise of salvation within a culture that is already saturated with meanings and materialism. Advertising – pointing towards, bearing witness to and proclaiming – is a fundamentally evangelistic art-science.[22]

It was, therefore, the commodification of meaning and identity through marketing that resulted in the decline of religious belief and practice. What good is the promise of happiness in the afterlife if consumerism provides it in the here-and-now on a regular and dependable basis?

The emergence of the commodified self also explains the development of Davie's 'vicarious religion'. In his *Engaging with Contemporary Culture*, Martyn Percy argues that within consumer culture religion becomes 'one of a number of "cultured" and "leisured" activities that individuals now purchase or subscribe to'.[23] Western piety has by and large become a form of boutique religiosity in which beliefs and religious practices augment individual identities and lifestyles. We can avail ourselves of various religious practices, such as attending church, as and for however long we see fit. Consequently, a few committed churchgoers provide the Church's services for the wider public to enjoy without commitment or obligation. Indeed, as Davie points out, throughout Europe people perceive churches as 'public utilities for the common good'.[24] This perception obviously fits neatly into a consumer mindset; the Church offers services for personal well-being alongside many other wellness providers. But to be successful in this, churches must be both relevant and places where people will feel good. Davie writes:

> What then is the common feature of these very different stories? It is, I think, the experiential or 'feel-good' factor, whether this be expressed in charismatic worship, in the Alpha weekend, in the tranquillity of cathedral evensong or in a special cathedral occasion . . . The point is that we *feel* something; we *experience* the sacred, the set apart . . . If we feel nothing, we are much less likely to be attracted.[25]

Orchestrating the event or spectacle – be it worship, a concert, emotive testimony, Taizé chant or an Alpha weekend – where people will have a memorable experience becomes essential to a church's success.

Brown's and Davie's research suggests that from the 1960s the Church could manage little more than to respond to societal changes; it had otherwise lost the ability to initiate or resist those changes. Increasingly, since the Church could not influence society in any meaningful way, it focused more on changing itself, normally in order to become more relevant to the surrounding society. The Church's inward focus coincided with the rise of self-actualization: just when people began to search for happiness through a self-invented authenticity apart from external influences, the Church began to search for success through achieving an 'authentic' voice apart from perceived foreign influences (patriarchy, colonialism, racism, institutionalism, etc.). As in consumer culture, identity and the acceptance of lifestyles became a primary concern of church life.

The Church consumed

Part of the reason why the Church has not very successfully resisted consumerism has to do with its prior acquiescence to the post-Enlightenment privatization of religion. During the eighteenth and nineteenth centuries, the Christian faith was increasingly presented in terms of an individual's subjective encounter with God and his or her subscription to particular doctrines. Likewise, the Church struggled to respond to those aspects of the scientific revolution, such as evolutionary biology, that appeared to challenge fundamental Christian doctrines. Ironically, by the time mainstream Christianity had begun to come to terms with high modernity, Western societies had begun to abandon it. Like many others, Christians leaders were generally surprised by the rapid spread of consumer culture and, therefore, unable effectively to gauge its nature or impact. Indeed, many Christian thinkers were still locked in the debates of high modernity (such as the relation of theology to science) when the wider population of the Western world was out shopping and constructing their new lifestyles. Also, most of those new consumers were themselves Christians and quickly imported their consumerist concerns into the Church – and this was exacerbated by a perceived need for the Church to market itself to a world of self-actualizing seekers, though rarely understood in those terms.

Since then the churches in the West have been almost continually locked in disputes about identity and self-expression. This is not to imply that contemporary theological debates can be reduced to mere reflections of a world moving from production to consumption, from modernity to postmodernity. Without a doubt, important theological questions have been discussed during the past 50 years. But both the fact that particular issues (rather than others) have caused controversy and the manner in which those issues have been discussed characterize a Church moving into a new consumer age. In almost every controversy, the presenting issue was one of identity, relevancy and accessibility, discussed using (often clumsily) all the marketing techniques and strategies available. In many ways, these debates parallel the equally strong disputes between the older school of Freudian psychologists and the newer humanistic psychologists (as we saw in Chapter 1). In other words, the transition from a psychology that sought to manage a dangerous and dark inner self to one that sought to express and actualize an inherently good one was reflected theologically by a movement away from a church that sought to impose constraints on sinful humanity to one that now seeks to be inclusive and accepting of as many lifestyles as possible.

But even while the Church was caught up in heated debates (aided in no small part by media attention), the churches in the West were experiencing much more fundamental changes due less to policy decisions than to diminishing attendance and a fast-changing culture. Increasing numbers of Christians were reaching adulthood without any meaningful Christian formation and often with altogether different expectations about their faith than had been traditionally the case. In short, they had begun to approach the Church as consumers, which is to say as self-actualizing individuals loosely grouped into corporate lifestyles through a series of technological networks. One immediate consequence of this transition was the loosening of denominational loyalty: individuals became less concerned with a set of doctrines or theological approaches than with the experience particular congregations could offer. Although this transition happened much sooner in the USA than in the UK, in both countries people increasingly attended those churches that expressed their worship and teaching in consumerists' terms: that is, a comfortable environment and through video, pop-style praise music, branded courses and workshops, and lifestyle products. In the USA, large religious retail shops began to appear in suburban settings purveying a vast array of Bibles and devotional books, religious CDs, T-shirts, toys, games, home decorations, accessories, guidebooks, candles, video games and DVDs. Religious entrepreneurs swiftly discovered that they could earn vast profits by broadcasting the gospel on television (even on a daily basis) or through heavily promoted and marketed books and self-help programmes.[26]

In all this, the governing force is the market. Martyn Percy notes that the transition from religious obligation to religious consumption means that

> churches have discovered that they need to be much more savvy about how they shape and market themselves in the public sphere. There is no escaping the reality: the churches are in competition – for people's time, energy, attention, money and commitment.[27]

A little later, he continues:

> Increased mobility, globalization, and consumerism have infected and affected the churches, just as they have touched every other aspect of social life. Duty is dead; the customer is king. It is no surprise, therefore, to discover churches adopting a consumerist mentality and competing with one another for souls, members, or entering the marketplace itself and trying to convert tired customers into revitalized Christians.[28]

But one has to be careful not to place church authorities or decision-making bodies at a distance from consumerism. It was not that the churches 'discovered' the need to be savvier about shaping and marketing themselves, but rather that they began naturally to think in those terms as their membership became increasingly influenced by consumerism.

The growing confusion over the role of worship with evangelism provides one of the clearest illustrations of the dominance of the market within the Church. As we have seen, within a market-oriented society, self-expression is understood almost entirely in terms of marketing. The ability to grab attention through publicity determines both a person's societal status and the authenticity of his or her identity; honesty means promoting one's true self for public acceptance. This same understanding has come to inform evangelism, which by and large has been reduced to a set of techniques for advertising a church's 'authentic' image. At the congregational level, this typically means producing professionally designed brochures, advertising services in local media, setting up and managing a website, adopting a mission statement, and arranging the interior to convey a feeling of warmth and welcome. In other words, evangelism is really congregational self-promotion with the intent of attracting customers. This same approach can also be found at the national level, as seen, for example, in the press release about the Church of England's new logo:

> The Church of England is to adopt a corporate logo in an attempt to rid the Church of its muddled image and provide a 'common visual identity' for its 13,000 parishes ... The Rev. Eric Shegog said ... 'The Church is one of thousands of bodies competing for attention in the media market place and we have got to do it efficiently'. He said the Church sought a symbol that had 'gravitas with a contemporary feel'.[29]

One would be hard pressed to encompass so many consumer catch-words – 'corporate', 'logo', 'image', 'competing' 'media market place', 'efficiently' and 'contemporary' – in such a short statement.

Two consequences follow upon the confusion of evangelism with marketing and publicity: first, there is an emphasis on removing barriers that discourage people from availing themselves of the Church's services, and, second, those services become reduced to products. Gone are the old Evangelical tracts about sinners standing under divine judgement and in their place are colourful brochures about the personal benefits faith offers individuals and families. In a sense, the Church is turned into a franchise, with the local church functioning as a shop where customers may experience, or buy into, a purveyed gospel. Like a franchise, churches hope to inspire 'brand loyalty', which typically amounts in practical terms to little more than enticing people to attend more regularly. Indeed, in the USA it is not uncommon to merchandise the interior to ensure that visitors will have a familiar feeling when entering the building. But, importantly, that gospel-product itself is too nebulous and abstract for mass consumption unless it is translated into a felt experience; this is accomplished through worship.

One of the most striking features of worship within consumer culture is its heterogeneity. Even within the Church of England, which for most of its history was noteworthy for its 'common prayer', one may now shop among official liturgies – *Common Worship* (itself with a plurality of options) or the Book of Common Prayer – or among a myriad of additional liturgies such as other Anglican liturgies, *Novus Ordo*, so-called Celtic liturgies, feminist liturgies, thematic liturgies, and so on. The assumption is that liturgies must be in a form and style that will appeal to a segment of potential customers. So, whereas in the early Church, non-Christians were converted to, not by, the liturgy, now the experience of the worship itself is supposed to bear the weight of encouraging customer loyalty. Thus, the spectacle has also become a more apparent feature of liturgical practice as a combination of music, technology and programmes are all employed to provide a memorable and moving experience for the congregation: the 'feel-good factor' to which Davie points.

Consequently, liturgies have been commodified. For all the proper language about how liturgies are to form and shape the collective and individual identities of Christians, liturgical practice is increasingly subject to pre-existing, secular identities. As mentioned earlier, one aspect of consumerism is the plunder of cultural ideas and artefacts for the sake of a fabricated and individualized identity. Likewise, individuals and congregations pull what they like out of their cultural contexts (for example, Celtic prayers, plainsong chant, South American clay altarware, not to mention prayer, music, techniques and artefacts derived from non-Christian resources) to create a liturgical experience that is appealing to the kinds of people the congregation hopes to attract. This approach to liturgy is as subject to changing fashions as consumption-derived identities. Hence, it is no coincidence that the liturgy has become the battleground for contemporary conflicts within the Church.

The shape of a consumer church

One of the most fruitful ways to observe this dynamic in play is by turning to the underlying theology behind the 2004 report *Mission-shaped Church* and the Fresh Expressions initiative to which it gave rise. Both represent policy decisions by the national Church to 'incul-turate' the Church in order to reach people within consumer culture more effectively. Since 2004, there have been some very pointed critiques of *Mission-shaped Church* and Fresh Expressions, perhaps most notably and controversially by Andrew Davison and Alison Milbank in *For the Parish: A Critique of Fresh Expressions*.[30] Because of these discussions, there is neither the need nor the space to provide an overall evaluation of these two initiatives but only to show how, on their own terms, *Mission-shaped Church* and Fresh Expressions reveal a thoroughly consumerized understanding of the Church and its mission.

Mission-shaped Church begins with a statistical analysis of contemporary culture taken largely from the government report *Social Trends*. It draws attention to general trends of the past 30 years – noting changes in housing, employment patterns, mobility, family life, leisure time and societal cohesion – before concluding with a discussion of the 'power of networks'.[31] However, this statistical survey has the particular purpose of demonstrating why Sunday worship is no longer generally practical: according to the statistics cited, people are now too occupied with DIY, family time, travel and recreational sports to attend church on Sunday. Without analysing this data further, the authors then supplement the statistical survey with a short discussion of what it means to live in a fragmented and networked society, before finally concluding:

> There are two distinct social processes at work here. Community is increasingly being re-formed around networks, and people are less inclined to make lasting commitments. While the two are not unrelated, the first is a change in the structure of community, with which the Church must engage. The second is a corrosive force that the Church must resist, because it undermines all forms of community. Contemporary initiatives to plant the church, or to express it appropriately within Western culture, will need to establish social capital: ties of loyalty and faithfulness through Christ.[32]

This conclusion betrays two questionable assumptions that underpin the rest of the report. The first is that a networked and fragmented society is both morally neutral and enduring and, thus, a cultural phenomenon with which the Church must come to terms. In other words, the report does not question whether a network society is, in fact, humane and sustainable except in so far as it has resulted in a loss of 'social capital'. There is no sense whatsoever that the Church ought to present people with an alternative way of ordering their lives and communities.

Second and more problematically, a distinction is made between the structural changes in society and the growing problem of commitment, even though the authors admit that the two are somehow related. The report fails to consider whether the two phenomena may be inextricably intertwined – that society is fragmenting because people are more individualistic and less willing to commit, or (the other way round) that people are less willing to make lasting commitments because they have no meaningful sense of community in a fragmenting and networked society. In fact, *Mission-shaped Church* later re-emphasizes this distinction, stating, 'It is important to distinguish between "consumer society" (a term that describes the current shape of Western capitalist societies) and the ideology of "consumerism" (which can be seen as the dominant idolatry of those societies).'[33] Certainly, this is true, as far as it goes, but it is also true that each depends on the other. Instead, the authors seem to suggest that culture can be separated from the underlying society, in effect implying that any other kind of culture might be engendered within a consumer society. As will be seen shortly, this proposal mirrors the assumed divisibility of form from content that underlies the report's theology; in this case, the authors argue that the form of consumer society might feasibly contain a non-consumer culture. This distinction allows the authors to insist that the Church ought to resist the 'corrosive force' of individualism while engaging with a networked society that both underpins and develops from it. Absent is any sense that by adapting to the structural changes in consumer society, the Church may become less able to encourage enduring forms of social capital.

One of the reasons why *Mission-shaped Church* does not consider such possibilities is that the authors seem entirely oblivious to the role of marketing and corporations in the rise of consumerism. In fact, the words 'marketing', 'advertising' or 'corporations' never appear in the entire document, which is astonishing given its thesis that the Church must engage more effectively with consumer society. This means, among other things, that it never considers the influence of marketing, brands or corporate tribalism on late modern, Western society. It never asks why people have become segmented into networks of lifestyles or how dependent they may be on branded technology. Even in its section on 'consumer culture', *Mission-shaped Church* only notes the various features of consumerism as though they appeared out of thin air.[34] Consequently, there seems little awareness that by adjusting to a society of networked lifestyles, the Church runs the risk of adapting also to the world of marketing and corporate dominance. Consequently, *Mission-shaped Church* colludes with the consumer culture it judges idolatrous. Indeed, consumerism arguably underpins its whole proposal of repackaging the 'content' of the gospel into 'forms' that appeal to different tastes. The kingdom of God becomes a product and churches the loci of that product's marketing aimed at different lifestyles and interests: café church, Goth church, Celtic church, new monasticism, youth congregations, seeker church, and so on. Christianity becomes the Church of the Consumer Tribes.

It is perhaps telling that while words like 'marketing' and 'corporation' never appear in *Mission-shaped Church*, the word 'authentic' does so repeatedly. Recall that within consumer culture, 'authentic' is used to describe an 'honestly' presented self-image that is pursued (though never fully realized) by self-invention through the consumption of goods and services. Authenticity is a byword for the free expression of all that is good and desirable in the face of adverse societal pressures. Precisely the same dynamic is at play in *Mission-shaped Church*, only with 'fresh expressions' of church pursuing authenticity in the face of adverse ecclesiastical pressures. Repeatedly, the report implies that 'inherited' forms of church not only lack authenticity but also restrain others from pursuing it. In other words, the parochial system is like those traditional cultures presented as decidedly 'uncool' by marketing.[35] Once again the theme of the film *Footloose* appears.

For example, *Mission-shaped Church* begins its section on what it means to be 'post-denominational' by observing:

> Younger generations are moving from being ecumenical to being post-denominational. Surrounded by secularism, materialism, competing spiritual movements and other world religions, simply being authentic Christians seems sufficient to them. Add to this the mobility of younger generations, and possibilities of real choice about where to affiliate, and denominations per se

are not seen as desirable designer labels, only as different types
of clothing, most of which are not thought 'cool'.   (p. 25)

Notice the easy interchange between substance and image here: youth
supposedly desire 'authenticity' but search for it by relating to symbols
('labels') that conform to their notion of coolness. Presentation and
publicity are as integral to the authenticity of churches as to the
construction of individual, authentic identities. *Mission-shaped Church*
seems to accept blithely that any actual presentation of the Church
(i.e., the inherited Church) lacks such authenticity because it is
no longer a desirable designer label. The brand must be updated in
order to attract customers. Presumably, since coolness itself is not a
fixed phenomenon, the Church's brand must likewise continually be
updated in order to remain marketable. But because *Mission-shaped
Church* offers no consideration of the role of corporate marketing
within consumer culture, it can offer no commentary on how such
a malleable church can remain independent of the whims of the
consumer market. Subsequently, the Church's perceived authenticity
is both indistinguishable from lifestyle marketing and determined by
its resonance with underlying consumer identities.

The language of authenticity appears again when *Mission-Shaped
Church* confidently states, 'for church to connect gospel and church
with them [ordinary people], a fresh expression of church is needed,
so that they can find and enjoy authentic Christian community,
worship and living'.[36] The authors do not describe what they believe
an 'authentic Christian community' is other than a place where
ecclesiology is subsumed under mission.[37] But they invite the reader
to connect authenticity with a new way of expressing church that
connects with consumers. The corollary to this is that churches
that are not culturally relevant or that insist on traditional modes
of self-expression are somehow inauthentic. This easy coupling of
authenticity with the novel echoes the world of marketing in which
individuals are convinced that the newest fashions and the next product are essential for pursuing happiness.

Not surprisingly, Fresh Expressions, the offshoot of *Mission-
shaped Church*, has been accused of being deeply 'collusive with consumerism', appealing primarily to thoroughly 'bourgeois' individuals,
and employing 'rhetoric often borne of middle-class thirty-forty-
something age-group'.[38] Martyn Percy mentions that the term 'fresh'

itself implies a 'sell-by' date and he wonders whether it can remain eternally new and fresh or how long it will be before a distinction is made between traditional fresh expressions and fresh, fresh expressions.[39] All of this is to say that Fresh Expressions risks appealing primarily to people who have been baptized and confirmed into the cult of consumerism. It also risks both becoming a spiritual accessory for individuals pursuing their vocation-as-consumers and fitting God (however conceived) neatly into a programme of self-invention. The fact that the communities of worshippers that Fresh Expressions highlights in its own literature – for example, for Goths, skaters and coffee connoisseurs – are generally examples of consumer tribalism begs the question about who is 'shaping' whom. Indeed, 'coolness' is a running theme in much of its literature. In the end, the Church's authenticity latches on to and sanctions consumer identities: God affirms the lifestyle no matter how artificial it may be.

Now, if *Mission-shaped Church* and Fresh Expressions confined themselves to promoting ways of engaging consumerism in order to convert consumers to Christianity then their arguments would become less objectionable. The gospel does have to meet people where they are and engage them in terms they can understand. In other words, if 'fresh expressions of church' were renamed 'fresh expressions of evangelism' there would be much to say for it. But *Mission-shaped Church* precludes this possibility in how it understands worship and how it defines the Church: both are subordinated to the Church's mission.[40] This is probably due to two factors: first, a conception of mission that is influenced by marketing, and, second, a view that worship is a means of attracting regular clientele. Again, the patristic model is of evangelizing people to worship rather than by worship. In other words (to use the language of *Mission-shaped Church*), the divine mission is to convert people into and form them as a worshipping community; that is what it means to be incorporated into the kingdom of God. The goal of worship is God. Instead, the authors assume that worship is a tool for attracting people to become members of God's kingdom, which remains a somewhat nebulous concept divorced from both church and its worship. So, for example, *Mission-shaped Church* declares, 'No one kind of worship can attract, much less hold, a major proportion of the varied population of this country.'[41] But is the purpose of worship to attract? Elsewhere, it speaks approvingly of churches that 'deliberately want to widen the variety of worship that is offered, in order to connect with a more diverse range of people'.[42] Here, worship is both that which attracts and the thing to which people are attracted. It is both the advert and the product, not unlike brands that are purchased for their own sake. In order for worship to combine both roles, however, it must remain relevant to the surrounding culture; in other words, by the very terms of this conception, worship must adapt to consumerism or else become irrelevant to a society of consumers. Worship-style is inextricably linked to lifestyle, giving rise to homogeneous communities based on commodified identities.

The confusion of mission and worship highlights the weak ecclesi-ology of *Mission-shaped Church*. In a much commented upon statement, the report defines the Church in a striking manner:

> The Son of God expressed this mission in terms of the kingdom of God. The kingdom is a divine activity whereas the Church is a human community. Kingdom agenda and values are often more radical than church readily allows. In bringing the king-dom, God is on the move and the Church is always catching up with him. We join his mission. We should not invite him to join ours.[43]

This reduction of the Church to a mere human institution is deeply problematic for a number of reasons. First, it is theologically unsound; the New Testament repeatedly refers to the Church as the body of Christ. As Michael Ramsey states, 'Christ is defined . . . not as an isolated figure of Galilee and Judaea but as one whose people, dead and risen with Him, are His own humanity. The fact of Christ includes the fact of the Church.'[44] Second, Martyn Percy suggests that by describing the Church as nothing more than a human institution allows *Mission-shaped Church* to portray the institutional church as a barrier to an expression of a purer faith in a way that appeals to a post-institutional culture.[45] Third, it makes a sharp distinction between the 'divine' kingdom of God and the 'human' Church that is radically Protestant in its conception and a departure from received Anglican doctrine.[46]

Finally and (for our purposes) most crucially, this distinction between an ill-defined ideal and its human expression closely aligns ecclesiology with consumerism. The kingdom of God becomes a concept that can be expressed in many different forms, which may or may not bear any relation to an institutional church. It is an ideal or image alienated from any particular tradition and therefore easily repackaged to meet changing consumer demand. And because the ideal is free-floating, its expressions become the focus: one has constantly to adapt the expression of the Church to connect the ideal (the kingdom of God) with the surrounding culture: hence the emphasis on 'fresh'. The 'fresh expression', ostensibly only a sign pointing to a signified ideal, is actually of primary importance because it, rather than the ideal, is what appeals to people. In other words, the acceptance of teachings about God's kingdom is of less concern than the expression and articulation of that kingdom in a style that is fresh, innovative and resonant with consumer identities. In a world in which image is everything, the Church itself becomes an image; the underlying reality (as *Mission-shaped Church* defines it) remains distant, ill-defined and susceptible to niche marketing.

Christianity becomes akin to a car. The ideal of a car is manifested in a multitude of makes and an even greater number of models, each with a wide variety of options. People almost never shop for a machine that will get them from point A to point B, but for one that suits their tastes, expresses their style and comes with the options they most desire. Most of these factors depend heavily on how the car is marketed and the consumer tribe with which people most identify: one sees this clearly during televised sporting events in the USA when viewers are subjected to a barrage of macho commercials about pick-up trucks. *Mission-shaped Church* and Fresh Expressions view the kingdom of God like a car that should appear in many different makes and models that appeal to people's tastes and effectively reflect their underlying consumer identity. Fresh Expressions is, therefore, perfectly suited for a world of shoppers, malleable to consumer preferences and ideally situated to meet the demand for a religious experience within an overarching consumer culture.

In seeking to adapt to the surrounding culture, *Mission-shaped Church*, Fresh Expressions and, indeed, the Church have not generally faced the full scope of consumerism's impact. Hopefully, the preceding three chapters have demonstrated that consumerism is by no means a neutral phenomenon or properly a culture, in any organic sense of that word, but rather the result of deliberate policies pursued by corporate marketing to increase sales and profitability at the expense of local culture and the environment. Consumerism is, therefore, fundamentally inhumane and unsustainable. But it is also astonishingly adept at connecting with the underlying pattern of human existence. *Mission-shaped Church* and Fresh Expressions unwittingly bear testimony to the strength of that connection since they both advocate a church that latches onto underlying consumer identities. Moreover, because consumerism has seized the sacramental moments of life, it now connects with people in a more enduring way than does the Church and its rites even while it alienates those people from one another, their own traditions and the environment in which they live. Consumerism is the lens through which Christian sacraments are understood, which means that those sacraments are now at least one step removed from actual human life. As will be seen in the next chapter, the alienation of the sacraments from human life means that they, too, become susceptible to commodification within a commodified church.

5

Alienated sacraments

―――――◆•◆•◆―――――

After two or three generations, consumer culture has become a fundamental way of life by which people perceive their world, relate to
others, understand themselves and pursue happiness. This underlying
consumer identity has become so deeply entrenched that it embraces
people of faith and reshapes the faith to which they subscribe.
As Vincent Miller notes, 'As people were being trained to find fulfilment in consumption, they were also, in effect, being trained to bring
the habits and dispositions of the realm of consumption to more
traditional sources of meaning, including religion.'[1] Although there
are aspects of consumerism that prick consciences, there are too few
examples of church communities that actively resist consumer culture
in any meaningful way; increasing numbers, as we have now seen,
embrace it either unintentionally or in a deliberate attempt to be
relevant.

Because consumerism now shapes our understanding of the world
and our identities, everything must be translated into a consumer
idiom to have any impact on individuals or their networked communities. Almost everything must present itself in the marketplace,
advertising its wares and promising satisfaction, so that potential
customers may choose to give custom. So, parents exhaust themselves
physically, mentally and financially ensuring that their children will
find them and 'family time' as entertaining as their game console or
the Internet. The natural world is either promoted through advertising its health benefits or brought under corporate control (as, for
example, an adventure park) in order for people to value it, though
even then typically not without the benefit of goods purchased
from various outdoor shops. Education has been reoriented towards
job-skills training, brought under managerial control and made as
entertaining as possible in order to be considered worthwhile and
useful. Even the classics of literature are continually repackaged (or

promoted through spectacular events such as never-ending cycles of anniversaries or film adaptations) to attract potential customers to the point that Jane Austen now does battle with zombies.[2] The cumulative effect of such translations is to drain everything of its distinctive power and meaning; having been absorbed into consumerism, the main effect of most things is to promote an aspect of or lifestyle within the world market.

This phenomenon is no less true for the Church, as can be seen most clearly in the contemporary conduct of the sacraments. Each sacrament and its engendered culture has been translated into the idiom of consumerism so that even while sacramental grace is given inwardly, outwardly the cult of consumerism is promoted and reinforced. Within a consumer culture, the Christian sacraments have meaning only in so far as they are connected with and filtered through the quasi-sacraments of the consumer cult. This alienation of the everyday existence of individuals and their communities from the sacraments presents the Church with one of its greatest challenges. If the Church now finds itself not only set in the midst of a religion of consumerism but also conducting its own sacramental ministry mainly on terms acceptable to that religion, then it cannot long retain any identity apart from consumer culture – the Church then becomes merely a niche lifestyle within an overarching global market and can offer no meaningful alternative to the system that now dominates the Western world. The Church ceases to be the Church in any meaningful sense, instead becoming a pastiche of Christian arte-facts marketed to a dwindling number of people who yearn for some kind of religious experience.

The thought of the postliberal theologian Stanley Hauerwas provides a helpful way of understanding the present-day dynamic. In his influential *A Community of Character*, Hauerwas proposes that social ethics arise from and depend on a narrative community. He writes: 'Every social ethic involves a narrative, whether it is concerned with the formulation of basic principles of social organization and/or concrete policy alternatives.'[3] Hauerwas is arguing against the peculiar claim of modernity that beliefs and ethics can be lifted from a particular community and treated as universal, 'rational' truths. Using Hauerwas's idea of 'story formed communities', one can illustrate the role of the sacraments in a consumer society. The sacraments are part of a particular society that grows out of a particular narrative or tradition: Israel and Jesus' incarnation, ministry, death and resurrection, and two thousand years of church history. That sweeping narrative of God's mission to the world as witnessed in Scripture and the historic life of the Church is the fertile soil in which the sacraments are rooted. Separate the sacraments from that grand narrative and they no longer retain their original meaning. It is likewise absurd to expect people who are not part of a concrete church community and for whom the Church's narrative is foreign to derive a proper meaning from the sacraments. In the UK, most people have only the vaguest awareness of the biblical narrative that provides the Church with a particular identity. Their narrative and the Church's narrative only bump into each other at a few sacramental events (baptisms, weddings and funerals), resulting most often in awkward moments in which families and the regular congregation dance clumsily around each other as each gropes after different goals: the families for a memorable event and the congregation for new membership.

In this chapter, I will show how the sacraments have been disconnected from the context of their foundational narrative often in the name of outreach. Typically, defenders of this practice see the sacraments as located now in a neutral zone between the Church and the world where they can serve as access points in which churchgoer and non-churchgoer can meet and worship together. My contention is that no such neutral zone exists, so that disconnecting the sacraments from their original narrative results in their becoming rooted in another narrative: in our case, consumerism. Thus, at key moments when many Christians believe the Church is witnessing to a wider public, it is, in fact, reinforcing a consumer culture through the Church's own symbolic acts.

Baptism and confirmation

As Callum Brown's research indicates, both infant baptisms and confirmations have been in decline since 1958.[4] While the number of baptisms has dropped at a modest but steady rate, the confirmation of adolescents is on the verge of becoming extinct, suggesting that christenings have retained a cultural role within families that confirmations have not. At the same time that there are fewer baptisms and confirmations, Sunday school attendance has collapsed: in the 1950s, roughly 40 per cent of children attended Sunday school whereas today less than 10 per cent do.[5] Hardly any children attend Sunday services with any regularity or, if they do, it is typically at a very young age. In general, therefore, outside of church schools (where collective worship is still normal), the Church has lost almost all contact with children and teenagers.

In response to declining numbers of children, the Church of England has undertaken several initiatives either to entice children and families back to church on an occasional basis or to organize extracurricular activities where they may encounter the Christian faith in an entertaining way. Almost all Church of England parishes now have 'family worship' at least once a month, in which 'accessible' music and informal worship are directed at small children. Additionally, many churches (Anglican, Methodist and others) now conduct 'Messy Church', a Fresh Expressions initiative that combines teaching, songs and activities to teach children about the Bible. In a similar vein, various youth groups and ministries draw largely from US resources to express the Christian faith and 'values' through youth culture: music, parties, celebrities and multimedia. Altogether, a tremendous amount of energy and good intentions are put into engaging children and youth, but sadly without notable success on a national level. There is no indication that the decline in baptisms, church attendance and confirmations has abated in recent years. Indeed, a recent study suggests that young people are more alienated from the Church than ever.[6]

Even as the Church has tried to retain some connection with children and young families, it has allowed those connections to become disengaged from the Church's tradition and regular worshipping community. This alienation has often been a deliberate choice, part of the classically liberal conviction that values can be lifted out of the communities in which they are fostered and expressed in a rationalized fashion. Baptisms are often conducted for non-churchgoing families apart from the regular worshipping community; songs sung at collective worship bear little relation to what is sung in actual churches; children and teenagers are taught values (such as respect and self-belief) with no particular doctrinal foundation, and apart from the ecclesial narrative in which those values have been fostered; and many initiatives aimed at children prioritize entertainment and stimulation over engagement with a broader community, place and tradition. In his book on contemplative youth ministry, Mark Yaconelli notes that current practices treat children and teenagers as 'activity-consumers' and exile them to the 'margins of the congregation's worship life'.[7] As a result, the sacraments and the various initiatives to engage children are separated from any concrete worshipping community. They are events young children and their families periodically attend in the same way they attend other events aimed at children. It is, therefore, by no means uncommon for children to reach adulthood unfamiliar with the Eucharist, the interior of a church, any set prayers beyond the Lord's Prayer, or hymns other than those composed for children. In other words, their christening will have made little difference to their lives. For them, Christianity is a free-floating and abstract phenomenon that bears no discernible relation to anything tangible in their everyday lives. Most will not recall their baptism, will never have been confirmed, and will have experienced the Church only as small children in a way that is appealing to small children. It is no wonder that so many grow out of Christianity at the same time they grow out of Santa Claus.

Admittedly, the Church is in an impossible situation. Having failed to form parents (or now grandparents), it can no longer rely on them to raise their children within a worshipping community. Those children's faith must often now be fostered despite their parents rather than through their active co-operation. This is something the Church has never really tried to do on a wide scale and full credit should be given to those who have taken on this task. But ultimately it is incredibly difficult to succeed because children perceive that the Church is not a priority (except at key moments) in their parents' lives. Parents, for their part, typically send their small children to church events because they help them develop a sense of right and wrong, not because the Church is particularly meaningful for the parents themselves. Thus, churches are placed in an impossible situation: they depend on parents supporting their attempts to introduce children to Christianity without alienating those parents through too much emphasis on distinctly Christian doctrines and practices. Furthermore, children have little sense that their parents are part of the Church; 'church' is simply an altruistic agency within the village or neighbourhood to which a few children are sent for their own good. It exists outside and apart from their families and communities, a fact reinforced by the almost complete absence of the Church or religion from the digital ecosystem children increasingly inhabit.

All of this has left churches with little choice but to borrow from consumer culture in order to appeal to children and families. 'Messy Church' is one example of this. Since its inception in 2004, Messy Church has become a major phenomenon in British Christianity, with many churches and communities now supporting it with local volunteers. In many ways, there is little that is particularly innovative or problematic about Messy Church; although it combines songs and activities long since developed in programmes such as Vacation Bible School (VBS) in the USA, it has been spectacularly successful in engaging volunteers and attracting children. The problem with Messy Church is that, like other forms of fresh expressions, it is intended to be the Church for young children and families. So, whereas in the USA, VBS is only one piece of a larger picture about deepening children's involvement in their churches, in the UK Messy Church is meant to be the whole picture itself. Subsequently, Messy Church is the only example of the Church many children encounter and experience. Unlike the 'inherited' Church, however, Messy Church is itself a product, complete with its own logo and series of colourful books, which is marketed to consumers (children and young families) to meet a demand (to halt the loss of children from the Church). Finally, Messy Church is almost entirely divorced from any living tradition within the wider Church: lessons are 'non-denominational' in nature (to ensure wide consumption), songs drawn more from pop culture than from hymnody, and the initiative hardly related to the wider Church, except perhaps through the Messy Church network itself.

Divorce of the sacraments and youth ministry from life within an actual worshipping community causes them to become artificial to those people they seek to reach. Instead of situating the sacraments within a storied community that impacts people's identity, they are turned into occasions to be enjoyed within a consumer culture. Baptism and confirmation become special events; a wonderful day for the family involved to be sure, but often with no wider or more enduring significance. Children and youth ministries are disengaged from almost everything other than their own networks since they relate in only a minimal way to the local church and exist in the world only as one of a variety of extra-curricular activities for the young. In both cases, formation is hardly mentioned nor, for that matter, even practical, given the irregularity of attendance. In the end, children and youth are taught a few very basic lessons about Christianity without endangering their continuing initiation into and confirmation as consumers. Indeed, were the Church to expect more from parents in terms of commitment, both the demand for christenings and attendance at various children's ministries would probably drop even more precipitously than they have.

The Eucharist

In many ways, the celebration of the Eucharist is the one sacrament that has most successfully resisted consumerism. This is perhaps not entirely surprising since the Eucharist derives its central meaning from sacrifice and communion, two concepts at odds with the governing principles of consumer culture. This is not to say that the Eucharist has resisted consumerism altogether. We have already noted how worship as a whole has been turned into both a product and a sale's pitch meant to appeal to the surrounding cultural tastes. In most liturgical churches, however, this commodifying of worship has not touched the structure of the Eucharist – more often than not, it has led to its abandonment in favour of more 'accessible' forms of worship – but instead has largely been restricted to influencing the supporting music, decor and homiletics. To a degree, therefore, one can speak of consumerism latching onto an underlying eucharistic foundation rather than undermining it altogether.

The main problem with the Eucharist within a consumer world, however, is that it becomes another event one attends rather than the heart of the community from which one derives an identity. People attend eucharistic worship but generally have not been formed so as to relate that activity to the rest of their lives. The Eucharist is something external to their ordinary lives rather than the home to which they return; it exists apart from their normal lives and so impacts those lives minimally. This is less a problem with the Eucharist itself than with how the Eucharist is situated within the church community. What does the sacrament of communion mean to those who have little sense of a church community? Generally speaking, it only connects with people formed within a consumer culture in so far as it can provide them with a feeling.

Of course, people have rarely participated in the Eucharist for the reasons that liturgical scholars and theologians have wanted.

For many centuries, most people attended a Eucharist primarily as an audience and because they were required to do so. On the other hand, prior to the rise of consumer culture, the boundaries between the church community and the local community were less distinct and much more permeable, especially as almost all the festivities and public occasions in which people participated were fostered by the Church. For a large proportion of the population, therefore, the Church and its worship were central to their collective identity, though, for many, after the Reformation this was not a eucharistic identity. The strength of that identity is perhaps still barely discernible in the importance of major feasts (Harvest, Christmas and Easter) to local (especially rural) communities and in the desire of many to be wed or have their children baptized in the church where their parents and grandparents were baptized, married and/or buried.

The dislocation of eucharistic celebration from a concrete and 'story-formed' community partly explains the growing practice of 'open communion' or 'communion without baptism' within some parts of Anglicanism. Originating (like so much else) in California, open communion removes the perceived barrier of baptism as a requirement for receiving the eucharistic bread and wine. Advocates of open communion argue that a truly inclusive Church will welcome all people to sit around the table and partake of the sacrament. Often described as 'radical hospitality', the laudable logic behind open communion is that Christians ought to welcome the stranger to one's table. Without going into a long discussion of this proposal, a couple of things should be noted about how the practice of open communion illustrates the disembedding of the sacraments from a worshipping, narrative community.[8]

First, the movement towards open communion can only appear within a church that has already alienated baptism; once baptism becomes merely an event unrelated to the wider life of the individual or to the body of Christ, its traditional role as the 'gateway to the sacraments' becomes less coherent. If baptism does not begin (for small children) or complete (for adults) a process of both initiation into a tangible eucharistic community and conversion away from the world, then it no longer bears any discernible relation to the Eucharist. Each sacrament becomes a solitary rite that people attend rather than connected acts of a particular community – that is, the Church – out of which a Christian identity grows. As a result, open communion seems to be nothing more than a tool for mission, another means of reaching out to 'seekers' who might stop by for worship. If the goal is merely to make people feel welcomed and included, then a church might as well resort to any kind of worship or activity that provides that experience.

Second, the practice of open communion accords well with a culture that has a stronger sense of entitlement than of commitment. It is a sacramental practice for consumers, to be enjoyed completely on an individual's own terms and without any obligation. Indeed, advocates of open communion often assume that hospitality precludes obligation or (to put it differently) that to impose an obligation is an act of exclusion. Thus, as James Farwell notes, open communion is ideally suited for those who want instant gratification.[9] People are as free to come and go as in their various networks and when shopping or dining. Commitment to a particular community is considered exclusionary because it monopolizes people's choices, and this is unacceptable in a world of hyper-individualism and fluid networks. Open communion, therefore, encourages a sense of community that is loose-knit and formed only through the sharing of an experience, as at a music concert or a political rally. People attend a service, participate for the length of that event and then go on their way. Any sense of community that might develop from this will arise less from the sacrament itself than from how much the individuals enjoyed the company of strangers. This final point is particularly true if one believes that the Eucharist is only efficacious for those who through baptism have been incorporated by the Holy Spirit into the body of Christ.

Marriage

Many of the ways in which the sacrament of marriage has been transformed by consumerism have already been discussed in Chapter 3. As we saw there, the Christian ideal of mutual submission has been replaced by that of partnership, and the sacramental rite itself has become the apotheosis of consumerism. There is a remarkable lack of proper theology surrounding the sacrament of marriage in the Church of England, which is surprising given the theological problems that establishment creates for a church that celebrates its Catholic order. If marriage is, indeed, a sacrament then it is one for which the

Church of England does not insist on baptism as a prerequisite. Until relatively recently, however, clergy could safely assume that those who met the residential requirements to marry in their local church would have, as a matter of course, been christened there as infants. But this is obviously no longer the case. Likewise, the couple intending to marry can no longer be assumed to have any relationship with the local church at all, never mind see themselves as members of the wider Church. Probably in most cases, couples approach a local church to provide them with a service (the wedding) to which they have a right by law and for which they expect to pay a modest fee.

As a result, marriage has arguably been more seriously alienated from the Church than any other sacrament. Instead of being visible sacramental rites, weddings in the Church of England are another form of outreach and a somewhat effective way of marketing the local church. In this regard, it is telling that churches are increasingly involved in the wedding fairs that have become popular events for various companies to market their products and services, thus encouraging the spiralling costs of weddings. Many clergy have made efforts to salvage an impossible situation by providing marriage preparation courses; but, while these are perhaps the best that can be made of a bad situation, they again typically take place apart from the regular worshipping community. They are an extra service provided at no additional charge by clergy to people who otherwise play no meaningful part in the life of the Church. This situation has been exacerbated by the relaxation of residential requirements so that many weddings are now conducted for those who are not even part of the local community. If one can even speak of marriage as a sacrament, therefore, it is a sacrament in which local churches often play only a very limited role.

As with the Eucharist, one might argue that few couples have ever entered a Christian marriage with any inkling of the theology that defines it. But also like the Eucharist, this did not matter so much when the boundaries between the Church and a professedly Christian culture were less discernible. In the past, before the advent of modern technology, clergy could assume that the bride and groom would play some part in the life of the parish, however small, and be part of a local community (village, town or neighbourhood) in which the local church played a prominent role. These assumptions no longer pertain, and so churches are bound by assumptions that arose before the advent of consumerism and that make little sense, theologically, within consumer culture. The sacrament of marriage is now provided, encouraged and defined largely in consumer terms and rarely performed within a worshipping community for those who are part of that worshipping community. At best, weddings are a service provided by clergy for the local community that helps glue that society together; at worst, they are simply an essential means for churches to meet their financial obligations.

Holy Orders

During the Reformation, Protestant attacks on the perceived worldliness of medieval clergy arose from a conviction that those church leaders were failing to be faithful to the dictates of Scripture. Indeed, the worldliness of clergy was a dependable source of complaint well after the Reformation, often employed by later Puritans against parish clergy or Evangelical and Anglo-Catholic clergy against their colleagues. In each case, reformers strived to restore the ordained ministry to its original identity and purpose (however conceived) rather than 'retool' it for a post-feudal society. This can be seen clearly, for example, in *Sermon of the Plough*, in which Hugh Latimer argues forcefully for an ordering of society freed from medieval corruptions – especially prelacy – and according to evangelical principles.

Today, however, arguments about the nature of the ministry tend to be more about conformity to modern notions of leadership than about restoration to an Evangelical or Catholic standard. Part of the reason for this may be the conception of the Church as just a 'human institution' and thus not unlike the secular institutions that have come under managerial control. If what matters is that individuals come to have a faith in God and embrace Christian values (disembedded from a particular culture) then it is essential for clergy to engage with those priorities. As John Milbank has noted, the result is to conform Christianity to the marketplace:

> Christianity is reduced to a readily graspable product: the promise of a mysterious relationship with Jesus, the absolute authority of a printed book, the reduction of complex doctrine to formulas about atonement, a single punctual act of faith which is like an absolute banknote, redeemable in eternity. The point

is that as many people as possible should buy this product – the interrelations, the social practices of these people are more or less beside the point. Likewise, the habitats of these people, or their cultural styles.[10]

Once a church begins to abandon its own distinct identity, its clergy lose the foundation for their own identity; their typical mimicry of secular power blossoms into the wholesale absorption of a secular identity as a model for all clergy.

This assessment may seem wholly unfair to many considering how 'worldly' clergy have been in prior periods of history. But in some ways the reality is less important than the ideal. Even when clergy were aping feudal aristocracy, their conduct was considered by many to be a departure from the ideal, as can be seen, for example, in Lollard attacks on clerical privileges, the representation of corrupt clergy in *Piers Plowman*, and Chaucer's scathing portrayal of senior clergy alongside his much less noted but idealized parson in *The Canterbury Tales*. But only a very brave person would label a present-day clergy-manager armed with his or her iPad, business strategies and management techniques as 'worldly'. That is because the ideal has changed; our conception of the role and nature of clergy has been aligned with a customer-provider model of the Church that is perceived to be the most effective way to connect with consumer society. The model is no longer a nostalgic image of a godly parson but of a corporate manager who can efficiently create and meet public demand in order to sell products. As a result, the last two decades have seen a proliferation of books on church leadership and strategic church management that borrow wholesale from the business world to devise models of ministry retooled to meet popular demand in a swiftly changing world.

A much noted and influential example of this is Robin Gill and Derek Burke's *Strategic Church Leadership* in which a SWOT analysis is used to determine 'strategic planning' for the Church of England.[11] The SWOT analysis is a managerial auditing tool for developing strategies by considering four factors: Strengths, Weaknesses, Opportunities and Threats. It was first developed at Stanford University by the same research group that developed lifestyle marketing. Their overall argument is that church leadership must be redirected towards ideas of 'ownership rather than consensus, for vision rather than harmony and balance, for priorities rather than equality of distribution, and for accountability rather than maintenance'.[12] In order to achieve this, they propose importing into the Church various management techniques for measuring and benchmarking performance in order to enable leaders to set priorities that can then be shared, owned and developed by congregations for themselves.[13] Such management techniques would allow

> church leaders . . . to provide and foster vision – theological, moral, strategic – and to enable this vision to be realised by the whole church. It would be their job as strategic leaders to think, plan prayerfully, to coax, to monitor, to help others to learn, and, above all, to identify and enhance opportunities for qualitative and quantitative growth and to be firm about subsidised projects that do not promote growth.[14]

For them, the setting of priorities is a crucial technique 'for intelligent and effective leadership, whether in the church or any other large organization; it is no more than a structured way of making choices'.[15] They conclude that without such priorities and techniques the Church 'cannot deal with rapid change effectively and creatively'.[16] In other words, they believe that in order for the Church to remain relevant in a fast-changing society, it must adopt management techniques that will increase the efficiency of the Church's performance.

In a series of essays, Richard H. Roberts argues that Gill and Burke seriously mislead people by presenting the rationalization of the Church through the adoption of managerial techniques as 'value-free'.[17] According to Roberts, the imposition of managerialism on the Church of England reduces local clergy to 'living tools' of a top-down managerial hierarchy and creates a framework for a quantifiable audit culture that not only increases control but demoralizes clergy and local leaders.[18] Through such audit controls, however, local cultures are 'captured, rationalised, regularised and then redirected' by the management, who then present their constructed reality back to local leadership for acceptance, ownership and implementation.[19] Similarly, Malcolm Torry notes that it is difficult to measure the actual performance of clergy (as with teachers) so that qualitative audits are forced to rely mainly on consequences that typically take little note of situational factors. That a priest may be highly effective in one post and much less so in another suggests how difficult it is to assess performance.[20]

The adoption of managerialism by the Church encourages a ministry that generally conforms to consumerist notions of professionalism.[21] Parish clergy function as a kind of lower-middle management who oversee local franchises according to the centrally produced 'mission statement' to which they are beholden. Diocesan and national managers and experts employ various techniques – such as developing mission statements, instigating periodic reviews, requiring continuing education, offering workshops – to try to conform parish clergy to whatever model of management is currently in vogue. In a telling part of Gill and Burke's discussion, they lament that the Church of England continues to operate like a 'badly run 1960s company'.[22] Instead of questioning whether or to what degree the Church ought to operate like a company, they mimic corporate consumerism by advocating a more efficient kind of human resource management. To their mind, a fundamental problem of British churches is that somehow the managerial revolution of the 1970s and 1980s passed them by.

Lost in the appropriation of managerialism by the clergy is any semblance of the sacramentality of the priesthood. As with consumer lifestyles, the priestly ministry is disembedded from local culture and turned, like experts, into access points of a totalizing system. The ministry is a rationalized construct, susceptible to changing managerial philosophies, unable to connect meaningfully with a particular community. Their concept of ministry conforms to an imposed model (the rationalized manager) rather than arising from a religious tradition which they enact and embody. And because one cannot assess the impact of sacramental grace or pastoral care on a eucharistic community, those clergy thought successful will be those who are most effective in quantifiable activities: growing churches, efficiently managing funds and motivating people. As in the business world, the techniques of these people are inculcated in those training for leadership positions within the organization (that is, the Church). Consequently, the model of the Church becomes a highly managed organization in which local entrepreneurs (clergy) conform to an audit culture in order to market effectively an ideal (the kingdom of God) through goods and services (worship and ministry) that will appeal to the surrounding population. The Church and its ministry together become a reflection of corporate culture.

Healing and wholeness

One of the greatest changes within churches during the past few decades has been the growing interest in forms of spirituality. There is much to applaud about this development, especially in comparison to the rather stale forms of religiosity that pertained during the height of modernity. Indeed, one possible reason for the advent of the New Age movement was that Western churches had largely banished mysticism in their pursuit of rational expressions of the Christian faith. Sadly, however, a great deal of modern-day spirituality emphasizes both individuality over the communal and the inner life over outward acts of charity. The term spirituality carries more social cachet than the term religion; to many, the former suggests openness to psycho-emotional experiences while the latter suggests submission to an oppressive institution that restricts individual freedoms of self-expression. By and large, modern Christians conceive of healing and wholeness – symbolized within the Church in the rites of confession and unction – as the purpose of spirituality: people engage in contemplative practices, seek out spiritual experts, attend retreats and read works of spirituality in large part to pursue a sense of well-being or as an aid for developing an authentic identity. Spirituality is now almost entirely a bourgeois pastime. Many books on spirituality freely borrow from psychotherapy – especially the kind that underpins much of the philosophy of self-actualization – to suggest techniques for developing an authentic personality purportedly more closely connected to God. In such cases, spirituality becomes a form of social adjustment within a consumer culture and a means for pursuing the authentic, invented self for those uncomfortable with overt materialism. Spirituality is, in fact, often contrasted with materialism, typically in ways not entirely faithful to an incarnational faith such as Christianity.

One of the most vocal critics of this kind of spirituality has been Kenneth Leech, who observes that a great deal of spirituality is formed to suit a narcissistic culture. He writes:

> It is a spirituality of self-cultivation, of personal enlightenment, of heightened awareness. It is often more akin to classical gnosticism, with its concern for self-knowledge and illumination, than to the biblical tradition, with its stress on the salvation and

sanctification of a people. Much of this spiritualty is gnostic also in its commitment to a dualism of spirit and matter, and in its failure to understand the incarnational basis of Christian spiritual formation ... Again, such current spirituality seems less concerned with the transformation of our lives in and through the incarnate Word than with the provision of comfort, reassurance and inner peace.[23]

This kind of spirituality, the roots of which go back to the various boutique spiritualities of the late nineteenth and early twentieth centuries, is a creature more of consumerism than of the Church, as can be seen by how casually much of it can lift distinct Christian practices (for example, Hesychastic prayer, Ignatian contemplation, Benedictine routines, and charismatic tongues) out of their traditions and combine them with psychiatric techniques (journalling, artistry, etc.) or practices from other religions (like Zen Buddhism) to form an appealing pastiche aimed at individuals more than communities. Almost never do these presentations of a spiritual life require a commitment to any particular community; they are for individuals to enjoy according to their tastes.

This kind of boutique spirituality has become one of the chief means (other than psychotherapy) for Christians to seek psychic wholeness. It is an approach to religion that is typically more interested in what a faith offers an individual than in how it enables individuals to offer themselves to God and the church community. In other words, spirituality is often a means to an end (well-being) rather than the communal environment in which people struggle with sin or celebrate God's blessings, perform outward acts of charity, form relationships, worship and work. Like the other sacraments, therefore, the ministry of healing and wholeness as represented by spirituality has largely become part of a consumer culture, often springing from the same sources, and consequently compelling churches to conform or lose access to the market. Often, in fact, Christian spirituality is subject to the same ebb and flow of fashion as found among brand-named products so that, for example, Benedictine spirituality may give way to Ignatian, Celtic or Franciscan spiritualities, or the labyrinth may yield in popularity to the Enneagram, journalling or quiet gardens. In each case, a 'type' of spirituality becomes situated within the framework of self-actualization and is typically marketed in terms of developing authentic identities apart from the deleterious influences of society.

An advertisement for a conference at Kanuga Conference Center outside Hendersonville, North Carolina, illustrates this point well. Entitled, 'The Power to Change: The Enneagram and the Emerging Consciousness', it advertises its subject in terms typical of consumerism:

> The Enneagram is an ancient spiritual tool for self-discovery that uses a method of personality typing and dynamics to reveal profound insights into our personalities. This study familiarizes us with the fact that our egos can blind even the holiest of us to the divine. The Enneagram illustrates to each individual how they can conceive of themselves not as an ego role but as an immortal being, divine intelligence and overflowing love.[24]

In many ways, what is important to note here is less the use of the Enneagram itself – which may provide useful psychological insights – than the language used to promote it. Spirituality is reduced to a 'tool for self-discovery' that draws on psychological 'typing' to reveal buried aspects about individual personalities so that practitioners can begin to conceive of themselves in the wholly positive terms ('immortal', 'divine' and 'overflowing love') promised by the exercise. There is no hint that the process might result in someone discovering that he or she is a cad. Indeed, the advertised result is not truly the self-discovery the programme purports to offer but an illustration of how the practitioners can 'conceive' of themselves in a positive light. Here, the Enneagram is basically a product advertised to a particular niche market that offers a kind of self-conceived happiness available to anyone willing to pay the fees. The promised happiness is presented in the form of an altogether consumerist ideal of well-being and wholeness (which epitomizes Leech's concerns about self-oriented spirituality), only now couched in terms of a spiritual exercise and promoted at a conference of one of The Episcopal Church's premier retreat centres.

The Kanuga advert demonstrates a common feature of contemporary forms of Christian spirituality: technique. The well-being it offers does not come through unmerited grace, works of charity, struggle with Scripture, or a long process of formation within a church community, but through developing proficiency with a 'spiritual tool of self-discovery'. On the face of it, there is no reason why the unbaptized cannot employ such techniques any less successfully than the baptized. The same is characteristic of many other kinds of spiritual practices, most of which helpfully provide step-by-step guides so that the proficient practitioner may achieve a sense of well-being. For example, people interested in contemplative prayer may be advised about posture, breathing techniques and the use of aids such as candles, icons or centring words. This is not to say that these techniques are unimportant or unhelpful. But often the implication is that success depends more on developing technical expertise than on God's grace or formation and participation within a community. Thus, even something grounded in a particular tradition as solidly as Ignatian or Hesychastic prayer is lifted out of a particular community, turned into a rationalized procedure and promoted as a kind of DIY spirituality for the discerning consumer. The Church plays almost no meaningful role in this process. There is a world of difference between a community of Benedictine monks and a collection of disconnected individuals employing Benedictine wisdom to de-clutter their lives.

None of this should be read as critical of various devotional practices themselves, especially when those practices are conducted within the context of worship and ministry. It is the commodification of those practices that is problematic. In too many cases, various practices have been turned into a commodity that one may employ for a fee in the private pursuit of a consumer goal. Also, both the costs and the language used mean that such practices and programmes will only appeal or be available to a fairly narrow group of people: primarily educated, middle- and upper-class individuals. Indeed, there is very little by way of spirituality that is fostered among working-class people, which may speak both to the identities of those offering the programmes and to the limited scope for profit among that segment of the population.

In the course of the last two chapters, we have seen how deeply embedded the Church has become within consumer culture. But what does this mean in real terms? First, it means not only that church membership has declined precipitously during the past 50 years but also that the identity of many who remain has been deeply influenced by consumer culture. One cannot really speak of a church community as being separate from the wider consumer world; often it is far truer to speak of a Christian niche within an overall consumer market. In that sense, the glee of Richard Dawkins about the extremely nominal faith of many self-identified Christians is justified; many subscribe to a faith in which they have not been formed and which influences them much less than the consumer culture of which they are part. This will have important ramifications for the next chapters as we begin to try to conceive how the Church might exist on its own terms within a consumer society, because any discussions or debates held within the Church will be deeply influenced by the rhetoric and assumptions of a culture that now contains it. Second, the embedding of Western Christianity within consumerism means that it has no ground on which to stand apart from that consumerism to protest against the many ways that it destroys communities, destabilizes individuals and wreaks havoc on the environment. Our present approach to being a church colludes with the very mindset that results in that massive, global destruction. As long as the Church accepts the primacy of the self-actualizing individual within the ordering of society it will promote, even sanctify, an ideal that is dominated by global corporations, defined by marketing, and ultimately unsustainable in terms of families, communities and the natural environment. Thus, the Church owes it to the world to be true to itself rather than relevant to a deeply destructive culture and society.

6

The household of God

The New Testament image of the Church as the *oikos*, or household, of God offers a starting point for reclaiming the Church's identity from consumerism. *Oikos* is rich with potential meaning for our present context because the family household or home is where people develop their identity, their attachments to place, and their deepest relationships with people whose company for the most part they did not choose. The home is where we are allowed most to be ourselves but in a manner that connects us to others. The home is also inherently resistant to rationalization, refusing by its very nature to conform to overt forms of systematization. But above all else, the home satisfies the human instinct not just to be but also to belong, and so has the potential to get beneath the roots of consumerism to connect with the underlying human condition.

Roger Scruton's *Green Philosophy*[1] offers a recent and insightful treatment of *oikos* that can be used to discuss how the Church might be a true household in which Christians discover a social identity rather than part of a consumer culture where people are encouraged to invent a privatized one. Scruton uses the idea of the home as the foundation for his argument that only by giving people a sense of connection to their locality will they become more environmentally conscious. Key to this is his concept of *oikophilia*, or the love of home, which provides some important insights about how the Church might reclaim its own identity. In short, the Church's mission to the world can be fruitfully conceived as an invitation to people immersed in an inhumane consumer culture to become members of an ecclesial home where they may discover a new social identity established in love and directed towards God. In this respect, local churches might be conceived as placed communities where people are formed in love through liturgical worship, prayer, mutual affection and ministry to the world. In order to conceive of the Church as home, one must accept also the notion that the Church should be a society separated from the world: Augustine's City of God in the midst of a worldly, global city. This is implied in the scriptural use of *oikos* for the Church: to think of the Church as home is also to think of the world as not-home. This distinction is strikingly portrayed in the late second-century 'Letter to Diognetus', which memorably presents Christians as 'resident aliens' spread through the world but finding their true home in God.[2] While a strong distinction between a 'gathered church' and society in general has long been characteristic of the Free Church tradition, such a distinction is much harder to make for an established Church like the Church of England. However, if the parochial system is conceived as a family of families, it can manifest itself as the household of God in ways that can resist consumer culture much more effectively than other 'expressions' of church. But this will require the national Church to demonstrate greater willingness to test the boundaries of establishment. As with the political relations between the UK and the USA, it does little good if the special relationship between the Church of England and the State is mostly one-sided.

Some will find the conviction that the Church should consider itself to be a separate society unappealing since this requires distinguishing between *us* and *them*. This conviction runs counter to the inclusive theology that is rightly concerned that whenever a group is identified as the *other*, there is the risk and even likelihood that they will also be treated as abnormal. Part of the sad story of humanity is that few groups have been able to form a strong collective identity without identifying themselves against others: Greeks versus barbarians, Jews versus Gentiles, liberals versus conservatives, men versus women, and so forth. But to treat other people as one of us without their consent is just as much a use of power as treating them as abnormal; indeed, it is a manipulative form of bigotry since it still imposes a world-view and narrative on the other without acknowledging the fact. In other words, one party is still dictating the terms of the relationship for both parties. Since Christians are called to love their neighbours as themselves, surely this requires at a minimum taking those neighbours seriously as neighbours, as people other than ourselves, so that they may then be loved with all the love normally reserved for the self even when they, of their own free will, exclude and reject us. It is the very fact that the neighbour is other, often distressingly so (as the fallen Jew would have been to the good Samaritan), that gives Christian love its radical edge. Consequently, it is my conviction that the Church can only perform its ministry if it takes seriously this distinction between home and neighbour, not in a self-congratulatory or defensive way but as the grounds for truly loving others.

Oikos

Although the concepts of family and home have changed over the millennia and vary according to culture, they have remained in substance the central building blocks of human society since before the rise of civilizations themselves. Indeed, it is a social unit that transcends our species, as can be seen with bird nests, ant colonies, bear dens, animal territoriality, and so forth. The place either where one is reared or later where one lives with a mate and offspring is a received, instinctual form of imbuing space with meaning. Unlike a club, team, democratic association or a network, the concept of a home did not have to be invented or developed – it just was. To exist also means to dwell and to belong, typically within a place we consider home and with a unit we call family. The fundamental unit of humanity, therefore, is less the individual than the family placed in a home, whatever that may look like. While a growing number of households consist of only one person, the family unit remains the typical household in the UK, though, of course, these families now come in a variety of shapes and sizes. Moreover, many currently living alone are either in search of a partner or have survived one. Thus, despite the effects of hyper-individualism and the subsequent breakdown of communities, the family remains a central aspect of almost everyone's life.

At its most basic level, the home is the place or territory inhabited by a family, be it a tent, hut, villa, castle, suburban house, caravan or stately home. Likewise, home normally includes the local area in which people live and where they have formed memories and relationships; the boundaries of the family extend to include neighbouring families and individuals. This can be as small as an urban neighbourhood or a rural village or as large as a wide suburban area made local by car travel. Moreover, often the conflation of home and family is further defined by the dimension of time: before the car, most families lived within the same locale for at least a few generations. The conflation of home and family within a particular locality over generations typically fosters both a strong loyalty to one's community and a suspicion of strangers. Indeed, until recently, the world was generally divided between a small but familiar haven of 'us' set in the midst of a largely unknown and vaguely imagined world of 'them'.

The home is, therefore, a unique form of community. Theano Terkenli identifies three dimensions that define a home: place, historical time and society.[3] The dimension of place derives from 'the recurrent, regular investment of meaning in a context with which people personalize and identify through some measure of control'.[4] Home is created at the interface of the self with the world and is a formative part of the psychological distinction made between us and them, which is to say home and not-home. The dimension of historical time is central to the idea of home 'because habits that repetitively unfold in specific contexts differentiate these locales or circumstances from the rest of the known world'.[5] This repetition of activities in a particular place forms a local tradition in which individuals invest emotional worth that makes the home, in its ideal, a place of security and comfort. Finally, the social dimension arises from the formed circle of relationships within a particular space that 'validate' an individual as a human being. These three dimensions of home together endow people and communities with incredibly powerful forms of attachment, as can be seen, for example, in the case of tribalism or nationalism.

It is important, however, to remember that for all our romanticism, the home can also be an uncomfortable place. In their introduction to the *Cultural Geographies* issue on the home, Alison Blunt and Ann Varley write: 'As a space of belonging and alienation, intimacy and violence, desire and fear, the home is invested with meanings, emotions, experiences and relationships that lie at the heart of human life.'[6] This reminds us that homes can be anything but places of security or love. But even in their brokenness such places remain home, the place where people establish over time their fundamental identities and their formative relationships, which is why psychotherapy often takes people back to their childhood to address underlying problems that persist into the present. If anything, broken homes impart people with a yearning for the real thing, for a place that can be called a home in the fullest sense of the word.

Until the idea of home was diminished by the rise of self-reliance and individualism, it was typically considered to be the basic unit of society. One's identity as an individual normally depended on an imparted family identity often expressed in terms of either a patronym ('son of' or 'daughter of') or a locative name ('de Montfort', 'of Loxley', 'von Aschenbach'). It is still possible to detect this in parts of the north of England where the names of family members are often prefixed by the possessive pronoun 'our'. Because travel was limited, people typically lived their whole life in close proximity of their birth home and in daily relation to both 'nuclear' and extended family members. The conflation of family and place had two further consequences. First, it provided a perspective by which to understand the great events and movements of the world. Most people understood momentous news primarily through how it impacted the local community. One can see this most horrifically in the case of the Great Plague, which became real for most people only when the first neighbours were infected. Similarly, Eamon Duffy's wonderful book *The Voices of Morebath* depicts how the Reformation became a reality for a small Devonshire village only when their treasured parish roles and church goods were banned.[7] And, of course, war memorials throughout the UK continue to bear witness to how a distant war became a reality for local communities. In these cases, people did not stand at an objective distance from events experienced primarily through news media but experienced them locally as a particular home community: a home provided both an identity and a perspective.

Second, the existence of a family in a particular home region over time provided a tradition or a collection of stories that helped to define the local community and its members. People were raised immersed in gossip, tales of memorable characters and local events, and regional customs that created a sense of tradition. As a result, the world was not only divided into home and not-home but also our tradition and their traditions.

This pre-consumer culture understanding of home provides a wider context for the many appearances of homes or households in the New Testament. In his now classic *The First Urban Christians*, Wayne A. Meeks provides a discussion of the nature of the home in Pauline literature that illustrates why the metaphor of home is essential to a sound understanding of the Church. According to Meeks, the most common location for the assembly of Pauline groups was the household (*oikos*) as seen, for example, in the case of Lydia at Philippi. There are also several examples of Paul baptizing individuals with their entire household – again Lydia is an example, as is Stephanas in 1 Corinthians 1.16 – and of Christians identified by the household to which they belong such as in the list found in Romans 16.10–16. From these examples, Meeks concludes that the earliest Christian groups were 'thus linked with what was commonly regarded as the basic unity of society': the *oikos*.[8]

These references to households also distinguish 'household-based groups' from the wider local church and the Church catholic. Meeks describes these households as the nuclei of the basic cells of early Christianity.[9] These were not the present-day 'cell groups' that typify many Evangelical congregations but often much broader household gatherings that theoretically included immediate family, slaves, freed-men, hired workers and even clients. Thus, for example, the church in Corinth was a collection of converted households within a single urban setting rather than a single congregation of gathered individuals. When the Corinthian church met, it was as much a gathering of clans as a congregation of individuals, which may partly explain the divisions mentioned in 1 Corinthians. The adaptation of the early Church to the social structure of the Greco-Roman world had implications for the internal life of the Church and the way Christians related to the wider world. First, the earliest churches were 'inserted into or superimposed upon an existing network of relationships, both internal – kinship, *clientele*, and subordination – and external – ties of friendship and perhaps of occupation'.[10] Second, the Christian ideal of *koinonia* potentially caused friction by undermining the hierarch-ical nature of the classical *oikos*. Meeks surmises that the later Pauline epistles' attention to *peri oikonomias*, the ordering of the household, arose from conflicts provoked by the two different social orderings; this may be what originally inspired the concept of the Church as 'the *oikos* of God' in which husbands, wives, fathers, children and slaves had particular roles and identities.[11]

The description of the Church as either the 'household of faith' or the 'household of God' appears in a number of places.[12] In each case, the church community is assumed to order itself according to its own *peri oikonomias* or social ethic. Ephesians and 1 Timothy provide the best examples of this. First, Ephesians grounds its social ethic on a distinction between home and not-home. Before the Gentile

Christians had been saved, they were aliens to the 'commonwealth' of Israel and strangers to the covenant, but through the cross, both the Gentiles and the Jews have been made one people, a new humanity, each reconciled to God: 'So then you are no longer strangers and aliens, but you are citizens with the saints and members of the household of God, built upon the foundation of the apostles and prophets, with Christ Jesus himself as the cornerstone.'[13] This passage exemplifies Terkenli's description of the nature of home: the Gentiles were initially among the 'not-home' part of humanity estranged from God but through grace and faith have subsequently become members of God's home and estranged from the world; the loyalty they felt to their old home has been transferred to their new home, the Church. In other words, salvation is incorporation into a new home or household with its own social ethic. It is also a particular kind of home: 'In him the whole structure is joined together and grows into a holy temple in the Lord, in whom you also are built together spiritually into a dwelling place of God.'[14] In Christ the image of home and temple merge into one structure that is the household of God. For its part, 1 Timothy clearly bases its household code on the understanding that the Church is the proper home of Christians: 'so . . . you may know how one ought to behave in the household of God, which is the church of the living God, the pillar and bulwark of the truth'.[15] Again, the image of home and temple merge into a guiding metaphor of the Church as the household of God and this provides the context for the subsequent detailed description of domestic roles; the individual households of the Christians are reordered by the social ethic of the Church.

These passages present a fascinating picture of the Church that is far removed from much present-day ecclesiology. The earliest church was conceived as the true *oikos* of God in which various Christian households and individuals were united into a single home of God, also understood as a temple. The family of God was, therefore, a tangible and concrete reality for Pauline Christians that reordered even their own domestic life. Presumably, the bishop was like a *paterfamilias* of God's household, composed of various related Christian households; the episcopal office united household churches into a kind of ecclesial homeland that reshaped prior identities so that both Jewish and Gentile Christians ideally saw everything outside the *oikos* of God as alien, foreign and not-home. It should not, therefore, be surprising that some of the earliest Christian debates were over dietary restrictions: the image of the Church as the *oikos* of God would have been weakened had all Christians not dined together.

In many ways, the image of the Church as the household of God in which local clergy function as a kind of *paterfamilias* can still be seen in the traditional parish. For example, Chaucer portrays his Parson as a good man of religion who, though a 'poure persoun of a toun', is rich in 'hooly thought and werk'.[16] He is also a learned man who preaches and teaches the Gospel 'trewely'. He looks after the poor of his parish and visits, in all types of weather, those in sickness and 'meschief'. And he does not hire a curate to do his work while he himself goes to London to advance his career, but rather stays in his parish to teach more by example than by admonition; in short, his life is devoted entirely to the local community. While this is obviously an ideal, it tells us much about the intent of the medieval parish: the parson was supposed to serve the spiritual and physical needs of his local community. The condemnation of those who run off to the courts in London, thus neglecting their flocks, reinforces this ideal.

The same ideal appears in the Middle English *John Myrc: Instructions for Parish Priests*, which carefully lays out all the duties of the parish priest. Myrc begins by advising the priest to practise unstinting hospitality: 'Of mete and drynke thow moste be fre, / To pore and ryche by thy degree.'[17] He should teach his flock the articles of the faith, the seven sacraments, the Lord's Prayer, the Angelus, the Creed and how to behave in church, even when to kneel and stand. He has a number of natal responsibilities as well: instructing women to make their confession and receive communion before childbirth, midwives to handle premature births or complications with delivery, and parents to ensure their children are christened, provided with good godparents, brought to the bishop for confirmation, and finally married off properly.[18] Finally, Myrc writes that the priest should visit the sick by going immediately to their bedside to administer communion and, if necessary, shrive the penitent.[19] Myrc's vision of a medieval parish ministry is remarkable for how deeply it reaches into people's lives. In its ideal, the scope of priestly ministry contains everyone who calls the parish home. The priest's time and energy are devoted to providing for the spiritual and physical needs of his flock from cradle to grave. He is involved intimately in all the major moments of people's lives and, thus, part of the place, history and relationships that provide local individuals and families with a powerful sense of home.

All these qualities can be found 300 years later in George Herbert's portrayal of a reformed parson. Herbert's parson spends his days walking around his parish, blessing those he meets, conversing with them, taking an interest in their daily lives, and using the knowledge gleaned from these rounds in his sermons.[20] He is learned in Scripture and related subjects, and studies hard to apply his theology to the ordinary lives of his parishioners. He takes particular care of the poor, even occasionally inviting them into his own home for a meal.[21] He is called also to be a 'Lawyer, and a Physician'.[22] He fulfils the former role by hearing disputes like a judge and the latter by becoming learned in herbal lore. Like Myrc and Chaucer, Herbert wants the parson to concern himself almost solely with the lives of those in his immediate community: 'The Country Parson is not only a father to his flock, but also professeth himself thoroughly of the opinion, carrying it about with him as fully, as if he had begot the whole Parish.'[23] He is the *paterfamilias* of the local household of God.

Certainly, all too often the parson was too beholden to the local lord (like Mr Collins in Austen's *Pride and Prejudice*) or was dilatory in the performance of his duties; often clergy left impecunious curates to perform parish duties while they lived elsewhere or collected livings without concern for pastoral provisions. But in most cases, the local church was central to a local community's identity: not long after children were physically born in a household, they were reborn at the font into God's *oikos*. Particularly during the Middle Ages when Church and society coalesced, this provided people and their families with a powerful sense of belonging to a local place, local people and a local church household. That remained largely true until recent times, as the many memorials that cover the walls of parish churches demonstrate. Thus, the church building set in the midst of a local village or neighbourhood manifested in built form the New Testament merging of home and temple.

Oikophilia

The current implications of conceiving the Church as *oikos* or home becomes a little clearer if we next consider the idea of 'oikophilia', or love of home, as presented by Roger Scruton in his book *Green*

Philosophy: How to Think Seriously about the Planet. As the title indicates, Scruton's primary aim is to develop a philosophical outlook for a sustainable society and culture, which he does from an openly conservative viewpoint. But it is his discussion of *oikos* and what he terms oikophilia that is of interest because it suggests that the Church can only function as the *oikos* of God if it endows its members with a sense of attachment; the local church must feel like home if the alienation that so characterizes the contemporary Church is to be overcome.

Scruton begins by defining oikophilia as 'the love and feeling for home',[24] which he opposes to *oikophobia* (or the repudiation of the home), *technophilia* (love of rationalized systems), consumerism and the desire to spoil or desecrate.[25] In developing this basic definition, he addresses two contrasting cultural theories: that of Clifford Geertz and Ruth Benedict and that of evolutionary psychologists like John Toby and Leda Cosmides. Geertz and Benedict argue that human nature is transformed by social structures that produce common motives over generations and curb the human tendency towards self-interest.[26] Evolutionary psychologists, on the other hand, propose that culture is really an adaptation of basic biological impulses that were encoded in our individual psyches when human beings were still prehistoric hunter-gatherers.[27] In Scruton's opinion, these two theories exemplify the now venerable controversy

> between those who assimilate customs and states of mind to adaptations that we could conceivably share with other species, and those who emphasize what is distinctive in the human condition, and who believe there is a radical break in the scheme of things, represented by the transition from causality to freedom, or (less contentiously) from animal to person.[28]

He tries to resolve this debate by arguing that human beings have mixed motives for what they do, some of which arise from evolutionary beginnings and others from reason. Motives like fear of the dark, revulsion towards incest and the impulse to cling to mother are examples of instinctive motives, while guilt, shame, the love of beauty and a sense of justice are examples of rational or personal motives.[29] But some motives arise from both areas – Scruton proposes a capacity for sacrifice as a prime example – and, therefore, create a particularly strong motivational force; reason and instinct reinforce each other. Among these overlapping motivational forces is oikophilia: 'a motive that comprehends all our deepest attachments, and which spills out in the moral, aesthetic and spiritual emotions that transfigure our world, creating in the midst of our emergencies a shelter that future generations also may enjoy'.[30]

Scruton next cites the political philosophy of Edmund Burke to emphasize one particular aspect of the *oikos* that has obvious applications for the Church. He proposes that a properly oikophilic society is a vertical association of the dead, the living and the unborn in which the present generation is responsible to the future through its veneration of the dead, in particular 'our' dead. He argues:

> It is by expending on them [the dead] some part of our care . . . that we care also for the unborn. For we plant in our hearts the transgenerational view of society that is the best guarantee that we will moderate our present appetites in the interests of those who are yet to be.[31]

Tradition, therefore, creates a link between the past and the future by shaping the identity and responsibility of the present:

> The dead and our gratitude towards them are woven into the narrative of domestic love. Tender feelings towards ancestors and those of whom family stories are told prepare us to make room in our hearts for our successors, whose affections we wish to earn. We learn to circumscribe our demands, to see our place in things as part of a continuous chain of giving and receiving, and to recognize that the good things we inherit are not ours to spoil, but ours to use wisely and pass on.[32]

This concept of society, however, depends on an instinctive and rational attachment to place and community that encourages people to embrace unchosen obligations (to parents, family, place, community). Scruton concludes here:

> human beings, in their settled position, are animated by an attitude of oikophilia: the love of the *oikos*, which means not only the home but the people contained in it, and the surrounding settlements that endow that home with lasting contours and an enduring smile. The *oikos* is the place that is not just mine and yours but *ours*.[33]

Finally, Scruton reflects on the philosophical school of Edmund Husserl to explain how oikophilia accords with the human conception of reality. Our natural attitude towards the world, which we only know through interaction, is not one of explaining but of belonging.[34] Our motives, therefore, are governed less by the way the world is than by how we interact with and belong in that world. So, the vital concepts of human existence are not scientific ones expressed in terms of theories but concepts that are

> functional, moral, aesthetic and spiritual kinds, which have no place in the 'laws of nature'. For example, the concepts of house, tool, friend, home, music; the noble, the majestic, the sacred; legality, politeness, justice. To imagine reasoning beings who lived without such concepts, who never divided the world into friend and foe, sacred and profane, just and unjust, home and not home, is to image a race of inhuman creatures, to whom we could not relate as we relate to each other, I to I.[35]

He understands this to be a deeply personal approach to an individual's place in the world that underpins moral judgement. He concludes that belonging creates rooted relationships in which individuals invest in things of intrinsic rather than instrumental worth. Intrinsic value allows the human heart to stop its relentless activity and, at last, find rest in the *oikos*.[36] Oikophilia is ultimately the love of that which is intrinsically valuable, which is, to Scruton's mind, the fundamental yearning of humanity. He concludes:

> Oikophilia originates in our need for nurture and safety, but spreads out across our surroundings in more mysterious and less self-serving ways. It is a call to responsibility, and a rebuke to calculation. It tells us to love, and not to use; to respect, and not to exploit. It invites us to look on things in our 'homescape' as we look on persons, not as means only, but as ends in themselves.[37]

Scruton's concept of oikophilia is Augustinian. For Augustine, every person yearns for a state of secure happiness, where he or she can be filled with joy without ever growing bored or fearing its loss.[38] In his book *On Christian Teaching*, Augustine uses the image of a return journey to a homeland to illustrate his distinction between those things that may be used and those that may be enjoyed.[39] We are to use things with instrumental value and enjoy things of intrinsic value or, in Augustine's own words, 'Those which are to be used assist us and give us a boost, so to speak, as we press on towards happiness, so that we may reach and hold fast to the things which makes us happy . . . To enjoy something is to hold fast to it in love for its own sake.'[40] Only the homeland can be fully and truly enjoyed; for Augustine, that homeland, the true *oikos*, is God.

The Church as the oikos *of God*

The postliberal group of theologians such as George Lindbeck and Stanley Hauerwas have argued that the Church's teaching and social ethic only make sense when embedded within a concrete ecclesial community that has its own particular story or narrative. One can only really embrace the values of a community by belonging to it and being shaped by its stories. For Christians, this means belonging to a worshipping community that embodies and enacts the scriptural narrative. Our discussion of *oikos* and oikophilia, however, suggests that if the postliberal theologians are correct, then we should say even more precisely that for the Church to fulfil its role properly it must embody not just a community but that kind of community we call home. The teachings, practices and structure of the Church must, therefore, encourage individuals to think of the Church as their first home, as their *oikos*.

Ultimately, only in the home can people form an enduring and grounded identity because only in the home may they find the kind of attachment, security, relationships, place and stories that grasp people, heart, mind and soul. To use Terenkli's three aspects of home, only when local churches become placed communities of invested meaning and emotion, with a narrative history and enduring social relationships, can they begin to foster the kind of identity that can stand apart from consumer culture and point to something different and greater. Within the home one develops an identity not just as a particular individual but also with a particular group of people and in a particular place, and partly by bearing particular obligations. Who my family members are and how they conduct their lives deeply impacts who I am. The place where we share ourselves with each other – including the landscape, the local customs and our neighbours – influences how our relationships develop. Additionally, my capacity routinely both to be a husband and a father and to fulfil my daily and weekly responsibilities gradually shape who I am profoundly. My identity is all the stronger for this experience of home because that experience is rooted in the deeply human need to belong and be settled. In fact, oikophilia gives emotional, spiritual and psychological content to belonging and settlement. The oft-mentioned shallowness of consumer culture demonstrates that deep and enduring communities must develop organically over time among those often unchosen companions we love, learn to love or at least with whom we strive to be at peace.

The problem with so many discussions of churches as communities is that a community can be anything from a nation to a network. As networks and the so-called digital ecosystem demonstrate, a community does not even have to be attached to a place but can exist in the free-floating world of people's collective imagination. 'Community' is a concept too tenuous in its definition and, therefore, too open to the influence of consumer culture. Ultimately, this is the problem with Fresh Expressions, for it embraces 'community' in its less tangible and more facile sense. However, the *oikos* conceived as a particular family situated in a particular place is a kind of community that can subvert consumerism and provide people with a profound sense of belonging. It reorients people away from the muddle of globalized culture and anchors them in a locality and among people to whom they must relate face to face. It also introduces them to a tradition that venerates the dead, some whom we call saints, whose plaques cover our church walls, whose furniture and appointments decorate our churches, whose prayers and songs fill our books of worship, whose graves greet us in the churchyard, and (above all else) whose presence we share in the Eucharist. This company of the dead fosters a concern for those yet to come so that the Church does not become dominated by the tyranny of the living. The present Church is a mediator between the Church of ages past and the Church yet to come. But above all else, that tradition communicates the central story of the Christian *oikos* – namely, Scripture – as its stories and lessons are shared among children and adults, read in the liturgy, sung in hymns, enacted in ritual and expounded in sermons. In other words, in the local church (like any good home) stories are shared at that central domestic gathering, the meal, which we know better as the Eucharist. When done conscientiously and persistently, such activities impart to the baptized a profound and often unarticulated sense of the Church as *oikos* – a home of holiness that gathers together families and patiently draws them together into God's kingdom.

7

Principles for a domestic Church

Reclaiming the Church's fundamental identity as our homeland will not be an easy task. In many ways, we find ourselves at the start of the twenty-first century in a predicament not unlike that of the Renaissance and Reformation when reformers attempted to reclaim a largely extinct cultural identity. During the Renaissance, scholars and artists tried to escape the perceived barbarity of their surrounding medieval culture by modelling themselves and their thought on the classical world. Similarly, during the Reformation, reformers such as Luther and Calvin sought to liberate the Church from the medieval papacy by turning to Scripture and the so-called Apostolic Church. They believed that only by restoring the Church to a position of continuity with the earliest Christians could it begin to be a truly holy community. But neither the Renaissance humanists nor the Protestant reformers could appeal to an identity or culture in which they themselves had been formed. Petrarch may have idolised classical thought, but he himself was not an ancient Greek or Roman; Luther may have provided a vision for what would become Lutheranism but he himself was not raised a Lutheran. This would seem obvious. But it means that both Renaissance scholars and Protestant reformers promoted an ideal community that was foreign to everyone including themselves. Neither group had ever experienced that communal identity as insiders for whom that culture was natural and unreflective. With the luxury of hindsight, we can see how truly medieval many of their reforms really were, shaped as much by medieval modes of thought and prejudices as by anything classical or biblical. And yet, neither the Renaissance nor the Reformation would have happened had they not attempted to reject the perceived abuses of their own late medieval culture by embracing their best understanding of humane civilization and religion. The birth of the modern world began in a deliberate attempt not so much to innovate as to return to a more pristine, pre-medieval civilization or church.

We are faced with a similar quandary: how do we discern what it means to be the household of God apart from the cult of consumerism in which our identities have been largely formed? How do chronic consumers imagine a community that is not based on consumption? Hauerwas's argument that social ethics arise from and depend on an underlying narrative community helps to clarify our predicament. The social ethic to which most of us adhere is rooted in consumerism and yet in order to reclaim the Church's identity we must try to embrace a social ethic that finds its source outside of consumer culture; we must, therefore, find our home in a place that feels foreign. We may discover that identity on a rational level through study, just as one may learn about a foreign culture by reading its guidebooks, enjoying its cuisine, studying its history, and surveying its literature, but that is a far cry from growing up and living within that culture. Thus, the greatest difficulty confronting the Church is how to embrace and foster a meaningful sense of being the household of God when several generations of Christians in the Western world have been formed within consumer culture.

The only viable solution to this problem is for the Church to re-establish the connection between its own story and symbols and the fundamental pattern of human existence. As we have seen in the first part of this book, the cult of consumerism has become pervasive because it has situated itself within the enduring patterns of life traditionally demarcated by the sacraments. Likewise, in Chapter 5 we saw how the Church, often without much reflection, has allowed its own sacramental practices to be subverted by the underlying consumer identity that shapes Christians and non-Christians alike. This is why the concept of the Church as home – as the place where Christians discover both a collective and individual vocation and identity – is such a rich model; the Church must relearn how to make the same kind of claims of allegiance on individuals and communities as did the earliest Church during the most hostile moments of Roman oppression. Only by encouraging that initial allegiance – understood as a claim to primary identity within the community of the Church rather than within the cult of consumerism – can the Church offer a gospel that both challenges and resists the destructive narrative of consumerism. To put it boldly, the Church needs to get back into the business of creating culture rather than reacting to it.

Rowan Williams provides a useful discussion about how a resistance that arises from faithfulness to the Church's own story helps to connect the Church with its own historical identity. He draws upon the earliest accounts of Christian martyrs to conclude that part of the Christian message is that sacral power resides in the Church rather than in the political world.[1] This conviction imbues the Church with the understanding that part of its role is to defy other claims to such power and authority.[2] Williams writes:

> The question of where holiness was to be found was an urgent and real issue in a society where holiness was almost universally believed to be located in political power: the pressure to define and refine, in ways that the modern student cannot immediately identify with, is not a light matter in such a world. And in the last century or so, it is significant that believers have from time to time had to confront just such pressure when the alliance of political power and a kind of religious mythology recreates something of the atmosphere of the Roman Empire. Thus when in 1936 the Confessing Church in Germany, the network of those who resisted the anti-Semitic legislation of the Third Reich, bound itself to the 'Barmen Declaration', affirming the sovereignty of God in Christ over all other claims to authority, the primitive shape of Christian self-definition became visible once more.[3]

Thus, Williams concludes, the Church will occasionally 'find its unity when it finds what it has to resist', by which he means that the accounts of martyrs during these periods help to remind the Church of its distinctive character.[4] In the context of consumerism, Williams's argument suggests that part of the way in which the Church demonstrates its holiness – its separateness from the world – is by being sufficiently faithful to its own narrative that its very presence becomes a visible challenge to the cult of consumerism.

Just as early Christians recognized that they were set in the midst of a pagan culture that claimed sacral power so too must we today begin to recognize the religious nature of consumerism and its claims on us. As we saw in Chapter 4, this has too often not been the case.

The desire for relevancy has frequently not been moderated by the recognition that the Western world has introduced a new religion every bit as pervasive and influential as the Greco-Roman religions that martyred early Christians. The rise of globalism, the growing dominance of corporations, and the increasing number of avenues and methods of marketing and advertising suggest that the hostility of the cult of consumerism towards any counter-gospel and its claim on identities will probably become more pronounced in coming years. Children today are far more exposed to consumer culture than children 20 years ago, thanks in no small part to the astonishing development of the Internet. The Church must, therefore, begin to take serious stock of its current predicament, clearly mark consumerism as a competing religion and begin the process of challenging it by being faithful to its own narrative, by seeking to convert people away from the cult of consumerism, and by reaching out in love to those most harmed by it.

The Church should, however, be careful about how it approaches this task. It would be a mistake to turn the Church into a kind of holy anti-consumer agency that uses the gospel to combat globalization and commercialization. An overreaction to one error often leads to the embrace of another. Fear of Pelagianism led some to take the doctrine of predestination further than Augustine (or Paul) ever imagined; a reaction to perceived medieval errors led to dramatic iconoclasm, intemperate rhetoric about the papacy, and the persecution and execution of Catholics; the fear of modernity gave rise to fundamentalism and Catholic traditionalism. In each case, those contesting a different practice or theology became inversely identified by what they rejected. Similarly, there is a danger of forming 'models of the Church' that are simply reactions to consumerism and thereby continue to define themselves with respect to consumerism. The Church must be more than a puritanical alternative to consumerism, just as it once was more than a Semitic alternative to Greco-Roman paganism.

Instead, the anti-consumerism of the Church should grow out of a deeper reality and identity whose internal logic and narrative lead to a way of life and world-view that by their nature resist and challenge consumerism. For example, in the Old Testament, Israel did not identify itself against human sacrifice but was formed as a covenanted community in which such sacrifices were considered repugnant. Early Christians did not identify themselves against libations to the emperor or blood sports but were part of a community in which such things were considered intolerable. Likewise, we must strive for both individual and corporate identities deep and rich enough that the pursuit of individualized and self-invented happiness through the purchase of goods and the resultant destruction of the environment become abhorrent. But because we are called to be in mission to the world, we must remain immersed in a world that for the foreseeable future will embrace consumerism and seek constantly to keep us locked into its world-view. The only way this can be achieved is for the Church to reclaim a robust identity of itself as the primary home of all who call themselves Christians.

In order to regain an identity apart from consumerism, the Church needs to take seriously the mechanics of evangelism and formation. The process of introducing people into the household of God should involve a conversion both to Christianity and away from the under-lying principles of the cult of consumerism. This might begin by clearly challenging ideas about self-invention, consumer lifestyle and pursuing happiness through the purchase of products, and by provid-ing an awareness of how these ideas impact people's live more than they are perhaps aware. To be effective, the wider Church should, therefore, seek to mark clearly those aspects of consumerism that are unacceptable to Christians, especially those beliefs and practices that harm human society and damage the environment. Similarly, local churches should think hard about how to make the rejection of consumerism easier for its members. In other words, the Church needs to begin to develop the same apologetic witness against the governing forces of the wider world as it conducted during the Roman Empire. Indeed, this witness against the cult of consumerism could be shared with other faiths.

Broadly speaking, the reclamation of an identity of the Church as the *oikos* of God will be best accomplished through fostering oiko-philia at all levels of the Church's life. Christians should be encouraged to see the Church with its narrative, worship and ministry of care as the homeland in which they settle and belong. The key here is a visible and enduring community in which individual identities can be formed and nurtured. At the local level, this domestic com-munity can be best achieved by emphasizing the three dimensions of a home – place, tradition and society – when ordering the Church's life and conducting its ministry to the local community. Church leaders should ask themselves how they can encourage people to become attached to the place, narrative and society of the Church. A good beginning would be for local churches to begin taking small steps towards beautifying the *place*, sharing the *tradition* and encouraging the *associations* that will transform them into ecclesial households. This is the work of renovation.

The three dimensions that define home can be further developed into five principles by which the Church and congregations can reclaim a clearer identity as the household of God apart from consumer culture. The Church should

1 be a discrete community that is faithful to its own tradition;
2 root its practice in a sacramental ministry that springs from a narrative tradition made visible through worship;
3 actively locate people within an ecclesial community by fostering corporate bonds of love and loyalty;
4 distinguish mission from worship and conversion from formation; and
5 willingly embrace martyrdom with grace and patient endurance.

If consumerism shapes people through quasi-sacramental events and processes, as I have contended, then the Church must find a way of regaining that lost sacramental ground if it is to make a meaningful impact on Christian lives.

Principles for a domestic church

1 A discrete community that is faithful to its own tradition

Attempts to conceive of the Church as a household should begin with the concrete and local church, rooted in a particular place and embracing a local community: the body of Christ fully present in the local makes visible the kingdom of God. The definition of locality here will differ according to place; while in a rural setting it will probably be the local village church, in urban and suburban settings it may be any one of a number of churches within a wider locality. The local church shares with the wider Church a formative tradition based in Scripture, linked through the Church's own story, and expressed through the lectionary, Bible studies, the liturgy, hymnody, the church calendar, and feasts and fasts. Any conception of the Church catholic should begin with the body of Christ manifested by concrete, local churches united through the sacraments and the episcopacy; the Church catholic is the ecclesial homeland inhabited by local ecclesial homes.

Key to developing such a community will be an articulation of the Church's identity as a discrete community rather than merely as an institution of modern society or of the State. As long as people continue to view their local churches primarily as agencies within their area, the Church will be incapable of forming those people into a discrete community. Agencies, almost by their very nature, stand apart from those who employ their services. Likewise, if local churches function as agencies, people will continue to avail themselves of their services – be they the sacraments, pastoral care, social events or children's activities – without any meaningful sense of belonging to the Church. To a degree, this will require parish churches to become a little more like gathered communities, devoting energy and attention to transforming the regular worshipping community into a coherent family with a strong sense of its own identity as the household of God. Although an indistinct boundary between the worshipping congregation and the surrounding community made much sense within so-called Christendom, it is less defensible in a secularized, consumer culture. Increasingly, the local community is less a part of the penumbra of the local church than the locale of that church's missionary activity. Developing more coherent congregational identities simply recognizes the changed cultural situation in which the Church now conducts its ministry.

A discrete Christian identity depends almost entirely on a meaningful process of formation. It is long past time for the Church to recognize that identities, including those of its own members, are being formed within the cult of consumerism and beyond the reach of Scripture. If, as we saw in Chapter 2, most children and young adults are in a process of baptism and confirmation into the consumer culture, then the Church is faced with the problem of its own members owing a fundamental allegiance to that culture rather than to the Church. We need, therefore, to devote far more resources towards providing serious education for both those entering the Church and those who are already members. A Church that rightly prizes the role of the laity in its governance ought also to emphasize the education of the laity in its own underlying narrative and doctrines. In short, we desperately need a revival of the catechetical process.

Finally, it would be helpful for churches to reflect on the ways in which the local can be better connected to the regional, national and global Church. There is probably a much larger role for regional bodies and initiatives for fostering a sense of a shared community than has so far been realized. The identity of any given congregation can be strengthened by an active relationship with surrounding congregations. Within the Church of England, there needs to be greater emphasis on shared life within deaneries than on synodical deliberations. This might be achieved through joint youth activities, occasional joint worship, fellowship, prayer groups, Bible studies, pulpit exchanges and pilgrimages. All of these could and should be conducted with ecumenical partners in the area. Such initiatives will have the additional benefit of providing some of these activities with a critical mass of participants often beyond any one parish with its small, active church community. Congregations with strong identities linked together through deaneries with strong, shared lives would potentially provide dioceses with identities that go beyond their central bureaucracies.

2 Christian faith and practice that are grounded in a sacramental ministry within a narrative tradition made visible through worship

The purpose of sacraments is to provide the grace and symbolic action from which the life and identity of the local church grows. They situate individuals within the life of the Church and the context of the Bible, most especially the life of Christ. Any use of the sacraments other than to perform those functions is fundamentally a misuse of them. There is no neutral ground between the Church's inner life and the everyday world where the sacraments may be situated as missionary events. Indeed, the sacraments have never been means of evangelism, let alone of promoting the Church to the world through the provision of sought-after events. People are evangelized to the sacraments, not by them. This last point needs to be better reflected by the actual practice of the Church. But what might this mean in practical terms?

117

Baptism and confirmation

One of the promising developments of recent times has been the reclamation by many churches of baptism as the sufficient means of entry into the body of Christ. All who have been baptized are brothers and sisters within the *oikos* of God and, thus, share equally in the task of building up God's kingdom. Baptism should be a rite of profound significance, oriented primarily towards the Church since it is the sacramental means of incorporation into the body of Christ and only secondarily towards the family of the baptized. Clergy should, therefore, stress to families that a commitment to the Church is expected for baptisms, with perhaps the non-sacramental 'Thanksgiving after Birth' offered to those unwilling to commit. The baptism of people with no meaningful connection to the Church and with no demonstrable intent of living out the faith into which they are baptized cheapens the sacrament. More than almost any other sacrament, baptism needs to be reclaimed as a sacrament rather than perpetuated as a cultural relic that retains a diminishing degree of affection within an increasingly unchurched world.

There needs also to be a greater emphasis on both baptism's connection to confirmation and confirmation's role in welcoming Christians as adults into the household of God. This could be accomplished by developing resources for children and teenagers that focus on rooting them in the scriptural narrative, the story of the Church, and acts of prayer and worship. Such material should seek to inculcate them into the community of the Church rather than provide them simply with a moral vision illustrated by a few Scriptural stories. Finally, confirmation is a sacramental rite of passage (in a world that has lost many such rites) and, as such, needs clearly to demarcate the line between initial formation and active participation in the Church. Part of Christian formation should, therefore, include the discussion of adult vocation within the Church. Likewise, it would probably be good for churches to rediscover ways of including children in adult worship (through, for example, reading lessons, serving at the altar, singing in the choir, and taking up the collection) rather than confining them to child-friendly services. The practice of integrating families into regular worship (as servers, readers, chalice-bearers, ushers and the like) common to most Episcopal churches in the USA could be a fruitful model for churches in the UK.

Eucharist

In his book *Being Consumed: Economics and Christian Desire*, William Cavanaugh argues that the Eucharist provides a powerful symbolic critique of consumerism. Whereas consumer culture is based on satisfying personal and self-oriented desires through the consumption of commodities, the Eucharist satisfies desire through the consumption of individuals into the body of Christ:

> The act of consumption is thereby turned inside out: instead of simply consuming the body of Christ, we are consumed by it . . . In the Christian view, we do not simply stand apart, as individuals, from the rest of creation – appropriating, consuming, and discarding. In the Eucharist we are absorbed into a larger body. The small individual self is de-centered and put in the context of a much wider community of participation with others in the divine life.[5]

By being consumed by the overflowing nature of God in the Eucharist, individuals are caught up into the body of Christ that transcends both time and space and settles the human heart within the infinite space of God's own love. In other words, the eucharistic community is the *oikos* for which the human heart longs; it provides the reality towards which the concrete community of the visible body of Christ points, however imperfectly.

It is for this reason that eucharistic liturgies have generally been developed in ways that bind communities together. In almost all cases, the first person singular yields to the first person plural; we do not come to God in the Eucharist as a collection of 'I's but as a united 'we'. Moreover, that uniting of individuals into a single body is both horizontal and vertical; it includes those in the past, present, and future in one single act of worship and communion. It is, therefore, important that the conduct of the Eucharist consciously include those two dimensions. In this regard, *Common Worship: Times and Seasons* is a wonderful resource for the Church of England since it provides liturgies and guidance for rooting the celebration of the Eucharist (and other services) within the narrative of the Church's tradition that encompasses many different times and cultures.

Eucharistic celebration should also be conducted in a way that distinguishes it clearly from the world without, of course, making it incomprehensible to the average worshipper. This, admittedly, runs counter to much received liturgical wisdom of the past 60 years, but it perhaps makes more sense if compared to a family meal. Family meals tend to be distinctive, incorporating small, domestic rituals and quirks of shared personalities that seem both to sum up the character of the family and to make meals intimate occasions. Similarly, special times of the year – such as Christmas, Easter or, in the USA, Thanksgiving – call for special meals with their own special rituals. The celebration of the Eucharist should likewise express the character and identity of the Church as the *oikos* of God in a way that marks it from other gatherings and, most especially, the world. It is arguably the most distinctive act of the Church and should be conducted in a way that reminds people that they have come into the heart of the *oikos*'s own enacted identity; the Eucharist is where the Church is most itself. Thus, the Eucharist should feel strange and foreign, though not unduly off-putting, to people not formed within the Church. Achieving this goal probably requires, among other things, training people to understand better the nature, purpose and ritual symbolism of the Eucharist. People often need help in becoming as comfortable with eucharistic meals as they are with their own family meals. When done properly, however, the Eucharist can become as much an anchor and expression of Christian identity as the family meal is for many family identities.

Marriage

Sacramental marriage is as much a sacrament of the Church as any other sacrament. This seemingly obvious point needs to be reiterated because it has come to be seen mostly as an institution that endures in its own right apart from the Church. If the Church is to rediscover its character as a homeland that locally manifests itself as a family of families, then the sacrament of marriage must be more tangibly oriented towards the Church. One step on the way to this goal might be for the wider Church to develop non-sacramental marriage services for those who may legally marry in a church building but who are not themselves committed Christians. This would allow for baptism to be restored as a prerequisite for sacramental marriage, which would clearly demarcate it as a state within the body of Christ. Similarly, conducting weddings within the context of a nuptial Eucharist (a normal practice in some provinces of the Anglican

Communion) would help sustain the central role of the Eucharist in the life of the Church and reinforce the idea of the Church as the household of God: partaking of the bread and wine as the first meal shared by a wedded couple symbolically roots their shared life within the eucharistic community.

Next, churches could consider ways of linking families together through shared activities, fellowship, service, and mutual care and support, without, of course, alienating those unmarried. Among the most successful churches are those that engage families as effectively as they do individuals. Families ought to form the backbone of churches and those participating in the worship of the Church should be encouraged to come together as a coherent whole. This will require also the Church confronting the problem of male participation, which has reached a lamentable state in many congregations. But reaching out to families should be done not solely or even chiefly through providing services and events for families but by encouraging them to work together for the good of the wider community. Activities such as sharing responsibility for children's work, serving at the altar, organizing meals and family events and looking after the elderly bind people together far better than passive attendance at family-oriented events. A collaborative ministry of families would provide a strong corporate foundation for realizing the Church as the *oikos* of God and for fostering a love of the Church as a home.

Holy Orders

Very little in the Church warrants more attention than the formation and role of clergy. The drive to professionalize the ordained ministry – which is now bleeding over into the training of laity – has proceeded with little true theological study. Kenneth Leech reminds us that 'Priesthood . . . is not a job but an identity, a condition, a state' that cannot be properly captured by any managerial theory.[6] The Church would, therefore, do well to examine seriously and thoughtfully the training and formation of clergy and the various models they are, often unknowingly, encouraged to adopt. There is far more to be said about this than there is room in this book. But in terms of thinking of the Church as the *oikos* of God, there are three main roles that clergy fulfil.

First, they are the enactors of the Church's own narrative. Through leading liturgical worship, preaching, administering the sacraments and pastoral care they focus a community's identity on the Church's primary story, Scripture, and enable that narrative to impact on people's lives. They are given authority by the Church to fulfil that role, and the laying on of hands in ordination provides them with the grace to perform it. They are 'walking sacraments'[7] whose ministry, grounded and enacting the biblical narrative, binds together the various families of the *oikos* of God into a single household.

Second, clergy should be facilitators of the Church's collective memory because they participate in a priesthood that transcends the present and is founded on Christ's own priesthood. Thus, the ideal of the priest found, for example, in Gregory the Great, Chaucer, Myrc and Herbert – visible also in Michael's Ramsey's gem, *The Christian Priest Today*[8] – should be adapted to meet the demands of the modern world rather than wholly cast aside as a relic of a by-gone age. Whenever the Church dismisses its own heritage, it risks diminishing its own incarnational character by breaking the visible, historical link between the Church of the present and of the past with the person of Jesus Christ. If there is a human nature and a fundamental pattern of human life that lie below various cultural manifestations, then it follows that those practices of the ministry that have endured through different ages and among different cultures potentially hold much wisdom for the present. We are not quite as different from our ancestors as we like to believe.

Finally, clergy should be conscious of their role within the *oikos* of God as the nurturers of oikophilia. In their daily rounds of pastoral care and in their preaching, clergy have a unique ability to shape the character of their congregations. Overly individualistic approaches to ministry can easily forget that the primary role of clergy is to their community and only secondarily to the individuals of that community. Clergy draw upon their training to foster a vision that enables congregations to understand themselves as the household of God. Above all else, they uphold that household in their daily prayers, offering its work, concerns and joys to God. Clergy are also chiefly responsible for encouraging and inspiring the laity to discover and pursue their vocations within the Church. It is by working, worshipping and praying together regularly over time that people will come to love and feel a deep loyalty to their churches. Only clergy are provided with the requisite training, sacramental grace and authority for fostering a corporate identity for local churches.

Healing and wholeness

While the promotion of the anointing of the sick and confession (both now unfamiliar to many members of the Church of England) should be a vital part of the Church's reclamation of its role in healing and wholeness, this section can be expanded to include the whole practice of devotion and spirituality since both have typically become oriented towards psychic well-being. One of the reasons why spirituality has been overtaken by the therapeutic culture (as both Rieff and Leech lament) is probably due to the rise of hyper-individualism during the twentieth century; in many ways, both privatized spirituality and therapy are technical ways of providing well-being in societies where fragmented communities are no longer up to the task. As Jesus' own ministry demonstrates, both healing and wholeness were once closely related to each other and understood in light of the community: when Jesus healed the sick, he also pronounced them 'whole', which meant that they could be reintegrated into Jewish society.

Now, no one would want to revive the same connection between personal morality and health that the gospel (and the Prayer Book's 'Visitation of the Sick') demonstrate, but nor should the Church settle for the privatized and commodified approach to health that predominates today. Both confession and the anointing of the sick remind people that their failings or problems have a social dimension, which means that they need not face those troubles alone. Bearing one another's burdens must be a salient feature of the Church as God's household; Christians should no more have to face crises alone than family members do; otherwise Paul's words, 'If one member suffers, all suffer together with it; if one member is honoured, all rejoice together with it', ring hollow.[9] Indeed, the way in which Christians love one another should be one of the most dramatic signs to the world of God's kingdom.

Christian spirituality, therefore, should be primarily social. It is less a tool for achieving a private sense of well-being than another way of describing corporate life in the Spirit. In other words, spirituality is first and foremost the experience of God's presence as discovered within the life of the Church as it prays, worships, proclaims the gospel and ministers to the world. Thus, for example, both medieval mysticism and early modern devotions grew out of a shared life within the Church rather than the individual need for well-being; indeed, within Anglicanism devotion was explicitly rooted in the *common prayer* of the Church, demonstrated by the Prayer Book's dual role as the Church's official liturgy and a manual for personal devotions. Likewise, various spiritual practices need to be better integrated into the Church's corporate life and rooted more clearly in its eucharistic worship. This really need be no more difficult than consciously relating various prayer groups, workshops, retreats, networks and pilgrimages constantly back to the Church's community, especially as found in worship and service, rather than to the practitioners' psychic well-being; like freedom, that well-being is best found in perfect service rather than spiritual consumption.

3 A self-understanding that locates people within an ecclesial community through personal commitment and the development of corporate bonds of love and loyalty

The local church can only function as an *oikos* if it is a placed community that fosters oikophilia; churches need to be more like families in which individuals participate than buildings where people attend worship and events. Obligation and commitment, both of which *Mission-shaped Church* recognizes as devalued goods within consumer culture, are integral to a sense of home. But obligations will only be freely accepted if Christians love their church and feel a sense of loyalty to its members. Church structures ought, therefore, both to encourage the creation of bonds of affection and to place expectations upon its members. Bonds of affection are developed through mutual care, fellowship and participation in the liturgy. Unchosen obligations might begin with strongly encouraging parishioners to attend worship regularly and participate actively in the life of the Church but should eventually include requirements for the reception of sacramental rites. Christians ought also to be encouraged to take seriously their obligation to love one another, especially those with whom they do not agree or particularly like.

Churches might likewise do well to promote or revive seasonal occasions (like Shrove Tuesday pancake meals, agricultural festivals, and Harvest Supper), which help connect people with the Church's tradition, the liturgical year and the seasonal activities of local communities. Bonds of love and loyalty are strongest when they bind together those of the present and those of the past. In other words, part of the Church's role is to resist the historical amnesia of consumerism by providing occasions that place people within the historical stream of the Church's own life and in their local area. Again, this is not dissimilar to the situation of the earliest Christians; part of Paul's ministry involved introducing the new converts to their biblical heritage. Paul takes pains to instruct his Gentile converts that the great men and women of the Old Testament are now their progenitors. For example, in his first letter to the Corinthians, he refers to the Hebrews in the wilderness as 'our ancestors', deliberately including the Gentile Christians of Corinth within the tradition of Israel.[10] In the same way, people need to be encouraged to see the Church's heritage as their own story and its great men and women as their own ancestors in faith. This is again a process of formation and education.

There should also be characteristics of the local church that help maintain the traditions that provide local communities with their distinctive characters. For example, a congregation worshipping in a rural parish might celebrate its agricultural heritage or one in a northern post-industrial parish its mining heritage. As discussed in Chapter 1, the Western world is now littered with villages and towns that are more shared environments than local communities. The decline of sources of so-called social capital – pubs, voluntary associations, annual events, local lore, and the like – has left many areas without any meaningful collective identity. By honouring and remembering a community's past, churches can play a crucial role in rebuilding local identity, especially in those areas where the collapse of industry or the influx of commuters has created a sense of rootlessness and fragmentation. Indeed, many villages and towns in Britain cry out for the kind of cohesion that churches provide in similar areas in the USA. Ultimately, one should be able to say of any given church that it is fitting that it is located where it is; churches that pay little or no heed to local customs and culture may risk disembedding themselves in much the same way as rationalized institutions and consumer culture itself.

4 A concept of mission in which evangelism is directed towards drawing people into a concrete worshipping community where they can be formed and sanctified

The confusion of worship with evangelism should be contested. In Chapter 4, I argued that an easy equation of the two has led often to an unmooring of liturgical worship in the pursuit of relevancy. The Church can only retain its distinctive identity apart from the surrounding culture as the *oikos* of God if it regains the conviction that the purpose of the Church's mission is to evangelize people *to worship* and not *by worship*. Like the sacraments, worship is not primarily (or even secondarily) a form of evangelism. Nor is it a well-presented event that aims to provide the kind of experience that will induce people to purchase the product (that is, the gospel) the Church is purveying. Like love and unlike evangelism, worship will not cease at the Second Coming; it is an act that transcends both time and place since it includes not just the living but also 'angels and archangels and all the company of heaven'. Evangelism is, therefore, an invitation (that may take any number of forms) to those outside the *oikos* of God to become part of that household and join in the eternal worship of God. In a sense, evangelism is the act of convincing people to move home; as in Ephesians 2, they are invited to settle in God's homeland, the Church, and to become 'resident aliens' to the world.

Participation in a worshipping community rather than personal acceptance of an abstract faith should, therefore, be the goal of evangelism. But if this goal is to be realized, the Church must give much more consideration to the question of formation. Communities are, by their very nature, unfamiliar and strange to outsiders. The solution is not to make the community less itself by removing anything that may be deemed exclusive but rather to provide a means for converts to become familiar and comfortable in their new home. This is probably particularly true of liturgical worship since it is not a typical activity of secular people. Thus, even when the liturgy conforms to everyday language, it remains foreign to those unused to any form of worship. Furthermore, since people often dislike what they do not understand, one can assume they will not respond well to words and images that conflict with their preconceptions, often shaped, it is well to remember, by consumer culture. For example, there is no reason that someone formed within the cult of consumerism should find the eucharistic language of death and sacrifice comprehensible. People can only really become familiar with the Church's worship through a process of formation into the act of worship. Much of this will be little more than their experiencing worship on a regular basis so that its words and rhythms can penetrate both hearts and minds. But it could also be bolstered by including within the formation of converts and anyone returning to the Church lessons about the purpose, nature, structure and goal of Christian worship.

Finally, by distinguishing between evangelism and worship, the Church can be less obsessed with the endless attempt of making worship appeal to the wider, ever-changing world. One of the gifts of liturgical worship is its tendency to become rote, which is really the point at which the mind becomes engaged contemplatively. Ever-changing liturgies force congregations to engage with them at a liminal level instead of participating in them at both the liminal and subliminal levels. Indeed, the symbolic acts of worship work primarily at the subconscious level. Allowing worship to be itself frees it from the burden of functioning as a tool of evangelism for which it was never devised. Worship and evangelism become discrete activities that form the twin pillars of the Church's activity in the world – evangelism leads to worship and worship enables evangelism.

5 An individual and corporate willingness to embrace martyrdom with grace and patient endurance

Finally, because any attempt by the Church to understand itself as the *oikos* of God apart from consumer culture will inevitably lead to criticism, Christians must be willing to embrace the modest forms of martyrdom that will undoubtedly arise. One of the greatest obstacles to the Church's witness is the fact that there is often no practical difference between Christians and non-Christians in the way that they conduct their everyday lives. The privatization of religious belief has led to a reticence to allow religious conviction to be seen to regulate public behaviour. Even in the USA where religion continues to play an important role in society, people are hesitant to ascribe their political or social beliefs to their religious convictions. But if the consumerism in which most people are formed does behave as a religion, then almost all political and social beliefs are based on religious conviction – it is only that these foundations are typically unacknowledged. Because of this, Christians should not only hold to their convictions but be seen and heard to hold to them in the public domain. In the introduction to his collection of lectures, Rowan Williams explains:

If it is true that religious commitment in general, and Christian faith in particular, are not a matter of vague philosophy but of unremitting challenge to what we think we know about human beings and their destiny, there is no reprieve from the task of working out how doctrine impacts on public life . . . If it is true that the world depends entirely on the free gift of God, and that the direct act and presence of God has uniquely appeared in history in the shape of a human life two millennia ago, this has implications for how we think about that world and about human life. The risk of blundering into unforeseen complexities can't be avoided; and the best thing to hope for is that at least some of the inevitable mistakes may be interesting enough (or simply big enough) for someone else to work out better responses.[11]

That we find this so difficult to do nowadays speaks not only to the defensiveness of many Christians in the face of societal opprobrium but also to our own diminished sense of belonging to an actual community; practising Christianity as a lifestyle choice within consumer culture does not provide a very firm foundation for challenging the ethics of that culture.

But crucially any angry response to the Church by consumer society should be greeted by Christians and the Church with grace, patient endurance and even joy. When Christians complain openly about being persecuted for their beliefs they empty their witness of its evangelical power. Very often when the Church speaks it is and will continue to be ignored. That is something Christians just have to accept, not least because there is little church leaders and governing bodies can say that commands overwhelming support of its own members. Patient endurance, one of the primary virtues of the various Epistles, should be encouraged probably more than it has been. Humility too is required because the Church so often has been wrong in its pronouncements and social convictions – though arguably not as often or as egregiously as its fiercest critics like to contend. But the true life, witness and character of the Church are revealed most powerfully not when we are proved correct but when Christians rejoice in the face of hatred and demonstrate love in the midst of persecution. The way the early martyrs won converts was not simply in their willingness to die for their beliefs but also in the way they met persecution and even death with joy. If Christians exhibit humility, patient endurance and joy then they are more likely to be forgiven when they turn out to be wrong than they are presently tolerated even when they are right.

It will be obvious to most people that these principles are difficult to uphold and require a degree of patience, prayer and hard work. But it is long past time for the Church in the West to open its eyes to the world in which it now ministers, to see how much it abets the very forces that have diminished its witness and to begin to be a home for those called by God into his kingdom. Consumerism is arguably one of the most destructive forces ever devised by human-kind; we are currently destroying the environment, traditional communities, and social goods on an unprecedented scale. Only when the Church is again the alternative to the dehumanizing forces in human society can it once more proclaim Christ crucified to a world that yearns, as it always has, for the generous and eternal embrace of God. At a low point in his life, when through his own actions Jacob had been cast out of his home, estranged from his family and forced to wander alone in strange lands, he had a vision in which angels ascended and descended on a heavenly ladder. The voice of God declared, 'Know that I am with you and will keep you wherever you go, and will bring you back to this land; for I will not leave you until I have done what I have promised you.'[12] May Jacob's response, made with fear and trembling, speak for our churches as well: 'How awesome is this place! It is none other than the house of God, and this is the gate of heaven.'[13]

Notes

1 The cult of consumerism

1 An exception is Steven Miles, *Consumerism – as a Way of Life* (London: Sage, 1998), p. 1. See also William T. Cavanaugh, *Being Consumed: Economics and Christian Desire* (Grand Rapids, MI: Eerdmans, 2008), p. 35.

2 On quasi-religious attitudes towards technology, see Heidi Campbell and Antonio C. La Pastina, 'How the iPhone Became Divine: New Media, Religion and the Intertextual Circulation of Meaning', *New Media & Society* 12:7 (2010), pp. 1197–207.

3 BBC, *The Century of the Self*, directed and produced by Adam Curtis, first broadcast in 2002.

4 Edward L. Bernays, 'Public Education for Democracy', *Annals of the American Academy of Political and Social Science* 198 (July 1938), p. 126.

5 For further discussion of connecting commodities with ideals, see Cavanaugh, *Being Consumed*, p. 17.

6 Arguably the key text for this new movement in psychology was Abraham Maslow's *Toward a Psychology of Being* (New York: D. Van Nostrand, 1962).

7 See, for example, Robert Reich, 'The Decline of the Public Good', 4 January 2012, <www.robertreich.org/post/15331903866> (accessed 10 February 2012).

8 On the influence of the Human Potential Movement, see Marion Goldman, *The American Soul Rush: Esalen and the Rise of Spiritual Privilege* (New York: New York University Press, 2012) and Walter Truett Anderson, *The Upstart Spring: Esalen and the Human Potential Movement, The First Twenty Years* (Boston, MA: Addison-Wesley, 1983).

9 Erik Larson, *The Naked Consumer: How our Private Lives Became Public Commodities* (New York: Henry Holt & Co., 1992).

10 Cavanaugh, *Being Consumed*, p. 34.

11 Cavanaugh, *Being Consumed*, p. 35.

12 For this and subsequent figures, 'Essential Facts of the Computer and Video Games Industry' (The Entertainment Software Association, 2011), at <www.theesa.com/facts/pdfs/ESA_EF_2011.pdf>.

13 On consumer tribes, see Bernard Cova, Robert Kozinets and Avi Shankar, *Consumer Tribes* (Oxford: Butterworth-Heinemann, 2007) and Michael Maffesoli, *The Time of the Tribes: The Decline of Individualism in Mass Society* (London: Sage, 1995).

14 The two standard works on network societies remain Jan van Dijk, *The Information Age: Social Aspects of New Media*, 3rd edn (London: Sage, 2012) and Manuel Castell, *The Rise of the Network Society*, 2nd edn (Chichester: John Wiley & Sons Ltd, 2007).

15 Miles, *Consumerism – as a Way of Life*, p. 53. See also David Chaney, 'Subtopia in Gateshead: The MetroCentre as a Cultural Form', *Theory, Culture & Society* 7 (1990), pp. 49–68.

16 See George Ritzer, *The McDonaldization of Society* (London: Sage, 2004).

2 Initiation into consumerism

1 J. Howard Beales III, 'Advertising to Kids and the FTC: A Regulatory Retrospective that Advises the Present', *George Mason Law Review* 12:4 (April 2004), pp. 873–94.

2 Public Law 96–252, 94 Stat. 374 (28 May 1980): 'Federal Trade Commission Improvements Act of 1980'.

3 'Marketing to Children: Trillion Dollar Kids', *The Economist*, 30 November 2006, <www.economist.com/node/8355035> (accessed 11 February 2012).

4 Julia Margo, Mike Dixon, Nick Pearce and Howard Reed, *Freedom's Orphans: Raising Youth in a Changing World* (London: Institute for Public Policy Research, 2006), p. 142.

5 Margo et al., *Freedom's Orphans*, p. 145.

6 Anna R. McAlister and T. Bettina Cornwell, 'Children's Brand Symbolism Understanding: Links to Theory of Mind and Executive Functioning', *Psychology and Marketing* 27:3 (March 2010), p. 224.

7 Margo et al., *Freedom's Orphans*, p. 144.

8 D. Buckingham, 'The Impact of the Commercial World on Children's Wellbeing: Report of an Independent Assessment' (London: DCSF/DCM, 2009), 5.5.

9 Alan France, Joanne Meredith and Graham Murdoch, 'Children and Marketing Literature: Final Report, CRSP 583' (Loughborough: CRSP, 2008), pp. 11–14.

10 See France et al., 'Children and Marketing Literature', p. 10.

11 Buckingham, 'Impact of the Commercial World', 6.17.

12 Margo et al., *Freedom's Orphans*, p. 148.

13 See France et al., 'Children and Marketing Literature', p. 7.

14 Jim Rosack, 'Brain Scans Reveal Physiology of ADHD', *Psychiatric News* 39:1 (2004), p. 26. See also Dimitri A. Christakis, Frederick J. Zimmerman, David L. DiGiuseppe and Carolyn A. McCarty, 'Early Television Exposure and Subsequent Attentional Problems in Children', *Pediatrics* 113 (2004), pp. 708–13.

15 On neuromarketing, see Patrick Renvoisé and Christophe Morin, *Neuromarketing: Understanding the 'Buy Buttons' in Your Customer's Brain*

(Nashville, TN: Thomas Nelson, 2010) and Erik Du Plessis, *The Branded Mind: What Neuroscience Really Tells Us about the Puzzle of the Brain and the Brand* (London: Kogan Page, 2011).

16 France et al., 'Children and Marketing Literature', p. iv.

17 On the influence of styles of parenthood on 'consumer socialization', see Les Carlson and Sanford Grossbart, 'Parental Style and Consumer Socialization', *Journal of Consumer Research* 15:1 (June 1988), pp. 77–94.

18 On 'Pre-adulthood', see Dan Kiley, *Peter Pan Syndrome: Men Who Have Never Grown Up* (New York: Avon Books, 1983); Gary Cross, *Men to Boys: The Making of Modern Immaturity* (New York: Cambridge University Press, 2008); Kay Hymowitz, *Manning Up: How the Rise of Women has Turned Men into Boys* (New York: Basic Books, 2011).

19 PBS (Public Broadcasting Service in the USA), 'Merchants of Cool', *Frontline*, 1 February 2001.

20 PBS, 'Merchants of Cool'. See also Amelia H. Arsenault and Manuel Castells, 'The Structure and Dynamics of Global Multi-Media Business Networks', *International Journal of Communication* 2 (2008), pp. 707–48, on how these networks both compete and co-operate through their various subsidiary companies to create a dominant global industry.

21 Sophie Herdman, 'Online Pornography: House of Commons Debate', *Psychologies*, 25 November 2010, <www.psychologies.co.uk/culture/house-of-commons-debate-online-pornography.html> (accessed 23 April 2012).

22 Branwell Johnson, 'Habbo research shows teens no longer join one tribe', *Marketing Weekly*, 10 January 2012, <www.marketingweek.co.uk/habbo-research-shows-teens-no-longer-join-one-tribe/3004729.article> (accessed 23 February 2012).

23 Margo et al., *Freedom's Orphans*, pp. 147–8.

24 See Jack Halpern, *Fame Junkies: The Hidden Truth Behind America's Favorite Addiction* (Boston, MA: Houghton Mifflin, 2007).

25 See, for example, Po Johnson and Ashley Merryman, 'The Creativity Crisis', *Newsweek*, 10 July 2010, <www.thedailybeast.com/newsweek/2010/07/10/the-creativity-crisis.html> (accessed 2 March 2012).

26 See Jaron Lanier, *You Are Not a Gadget* (London: Penguin, 2010), pp. 18, 24–44.

27 See, for example, Juliet B. Schor, *Born to Buy: The Commercialized Child and the New Consumer* (New York: Scribner, 2004), pp. 119–76; Margo et al., *Freedom's Orphans*, pp. 147–52.

28 *The Impact of the Commercial World on Children's Wellbeing: Report of an Independent Assessment for the Department for Children, Schools and Families and the Department for Culture, Media and Sport* (London: Department for Children, Schools and Families, 2010), 11.20, p. 96.

29 Margo et al., *Freedom's Orphans*, pp. 19–47.

3 The consumer rites of adulthood

1 Zygmunt Bauman, *Consuming Life* (Cambridge: Polity Press, 2011), p. 55.
2 Bauman, *Consuming Life*, p. 55.
3 Bauman, *Consuming Life*, p. 56.
4 See Bauman, *Consuming Life*, pp. 21–3.
5 On the wedding industry, see Rebecca Mead, *One Perfect Day: The Selling of the American Wedding* (New York: Penguin, 2008).
6 Oliver O'Donovan, *Common Objects of Love: Moral Reflection and the Shaping of Community* (Grand Rapids, MI: Eerdmans, 2002), pp. 58–9.
7 See, for example, Brené Brown, *The Gifts of Imperfection: Let Go of Who You Think You're Supposed to Be and Embrace Who You Are* (Center City, MN: Hazelden, 2010) and Mike Robbin, *Be Yourself, Everyone Else is Already Taken: Transform Your Life with the Power of Authenticity* (San Francisco, CA: Jossey-Bass, 2009).
8 See, for example, Christopher Lasch, *The Culture of Narcissism: American Life in an Age of Diminishing Expectations* (New York: W. W. Norton & Co., 1981).
9 Philip Rieff, *The Triumph of the Therapeutic: Uses of Faith after Freud* (Wilmington, DE: ISI Books, 2006).
10 Vincent Miller, *Consuming Religion: Christian Faith and Practice in a Consumer Culture* (London: Continuum, 2005), p. 85.
11 Rieff, *The Triumph of the Therapeutic*, pp. 40, 55–65.
12 Miller, *Consuming Religion*, 86.
13 See also John Ryan, William Wentworth and Gabrielle Chapman, 'Models of Emotions in Therapeutic Self-Help Books', *Sociological Spectrum* 14 (1994), pp. 241–55.
14 For a similar approach, see Alisdair McIntyre, *After Virtue* (South Bend, IN: University of Notre Dame Press, 2007).
15 George Ritzer, *The McDonaldization of Society* (London: Sage, 2004), pp. 14–16.
16 David Ulrich, *Human Resource Champions: The Next Agenda for Adding Value and Delivering Results* (Boston, MA: Harvard Business School, 1996), pp. 24–5.
17 Richard H. Roberts, 'Personhood and Performance: Managerialism, Post-Democracy and the Ethics of "Enrichment"', *Studies in Christian Ethics* 21:61 (2008), pp. 75–6.
18 Roberts, 'Personhood and Performance', p. 63.
19 Roberts, 'Personhood and Performance', pp. 67–8.
20 For the following discussion, see Anthony Giddens, *Consequences of Modernity* (Palo Alto, CA: Stanford University Press, 1990) and *Modernity*

and Self-Identity: Self and Society in the Late Modern Age (Palo Alto, CA: Stanford University Press, 2001), pp. 17–21.

21 Giddens, *Consequences of Modernity*, p. 85.

22 One of the first and most influential of these critiques is Daniel Boorstin, *The Image: A Guide to Pseudo-Events in America* (New York: Vintage Books, 1992).

23 Graeme Turner, *Understanding Celebrity* (London: Sage, 2004), p. 24.

24 Chris Rojek, *Celebrity* (London: Reaktion Books Ltd, 2001), p. 53.

25 Rojek, *Celebrity*, pp. 52–3.

26 Rojek, *Celebrity*, pp. 58–99.

27 Augustine, sermon 229.2 in Augustine, *Essential Sermons*, tr. Edmund Hill OP (Hyde Park, NY: New City Press, 2007).

28 Grant David McCracken, *Culture and Consumption* (Bloomington, IN: Indiana University Press, 1990), p. xi.

4 A Church for consumer tribes

1 Callum Brown, *The Death of Christian Britain* (London: Routledge, 2009), p. 192.

2 In the following chapters, analyses of Fresh Expressions will be concerned (in most cases) with the initiative within the Church of England. For more information about Fresh Expressions, see <www.freshexpressions.org>.

3 For an excellent analysis of this topic, see Oliver O'Donovan, *The Desire of the Nations: Rediscovering the Roots of Political Theology* (Cambridge: Cambridge University Press, 1996) and Oliver O'Donovan and Joan Lockwood O'Donovan (eds), *From Irenaeus to Grotius: A Sourcebook in Christian Political Thought* (Grand Rapids, MI: Eerdmans, 1999).

4 John William Parker (ed.), *Essays and Reviews* (London, 1860); *Soundings: Essays Concerning Christian Understanding* (Cambridge: Cambridge University Press, 1962).

5 Christine Rosen, *Preaching Eugenics: Religious Leaders and the American Eugenics Movement* (New York: Oxford University Press, 2004).

6 Brown, *Death of Christian Britain*, p. 170.

7 Brown, *Death of Christian Britain*, pp. 170–1.

8 Brown, *Death of Christian Britain*, p. 172.

9 Brown, *Death of Christian Britain*, p. 176.

10 Brown, *Death of Christian Britain*, pp. 176–7.

11 Brown, *Death of Christian Britain*, p. 179.

12 Brown, *Death of Christian Britain*, pp. 189–90.

13 Brown, *Death of Christian Britain*, p. 190.

14 Grace Davie, *Religion in Britain since 1945* (Oxford: Blackwell, 1994), p. 76.

15 Grace Davie, 'From Obligation to Consumption: A Framework for Reflection on Northern Europe', *Political Theology* 6:3 (2005), p. 285.

16 Davie, 'From Obligation to Consumption', pp. 288–9.

17 Davie, *Religion in Britain*, p. 53.

18 Davie, 'From Obligation to Consumption', p. 291.

19 Davie, 'From Obligation to Consumption', pp. 293–4.

20 Davie, *Religion in Britain*, p. 19.

21 Davie, *Religion in Britain*, p. 19.

22 Martyn Percy, *Engaging with Contemporary Culture: Christianity, Theology, and the Concrete Church* (Aldershot: Ashgate, 2005), p. 52.

23 Percy, *Engaging with Contemporary Culture*, p. 48.

24 Davie, 'From Obligation to Consumption', p. 290.

25 Davie, 'From Obligation to Consumption', p. 294.

26 R. Laurence Moore, *Selling God: American Religion in the Marketplace of Culture* (Oxford: Oxford University Press, 2004).

27 Percy, *Engaging with Contemporary Culture*, p. 47.

28 Percy, *Engaging with Contemporary Culture*, p. 48.

29 Quoted in Steven Miles, *Consumerism – as a Way of Life* (London: Sage, 1998), p. 1.

30 Andrew Davison and Alison Milbank, *For the Parish: A Critique of Fresh Expressions* (London: SCM Press, 2010).

31 *Mission-shaped Church: Church Planting and Fresh Expressions of Church in a Changing Context* (London: Church House Publishing, 2004), pp. 1–6.

32 *Mission-shaped Church*, p. 7.

33 *Mission-shaped Church*, p. 10.

34 *Mission-shaped Church*, pp. 9–11.

35 See Martyn Percy, 'Old Tricks for New Dogs? A Critique of Fresh Expressions' in L. Nelstrop and M. Percy (eds), *Evaluating Fresh Expressions* (Norwich: Canterbury Press, 2008), pp. 28–9.

36 *Mission-shaped Church*, p. 79.

37 See, for example, *Mission-shaped Church*, p. 24.

38 Percy, *Engaging with Contemporary Culture*, pp. 34–5.

39 Percy, *Engaging with Contemporary Culture*, p. 36.

40 See, for example, *Mission-shaped Church*, p. 62.

41 *Mission-shaped Church*, p. 13.

42 *Mission-shaped Church*, p. 61.

43 *Mission-shaped Church*, p. 86.

44 Michael Ramsey, *The Gospel and the Catholic Church* (London: Longmans, 1956), pp. 33–4.

45 Percy, *Engaging with Contemporary Culture*, p. 28.

46 Davison and Milbank, *For the Parish*, p. 41.

5 Alienated sacraments

1 Vincent Miller, *Consuming Religion: Christian Faith and Practice in a Consumer Culture* (London: Continuum, 2005), p. 88.

2 See Seth Grahame-Smith, *Pride and Prejudice and Zombies* (Philadelphia, PA: Quirk Books, 2009).

3 Stanley Hauerwas, *A Community of Character* (South Bend, IN: University of Notre Dame Press, 1981), p. 9.

4 See chart in Callum Brown, *The Death of Christian Britain* (London: Routledge, 2009), p. 168.

5 Brown, *Death of Christian Britain*, p. 168.

6 According to the 'British Social Attitudes' survey (28:182), 65 per cent of young people have no religious affiliation, which is 10 per cent higher than the national average (London: National Centre for Social Research, 2012).

7 Mark Yaconelli, *Growing Souls: Experiments in Contemplative Youth Ministry* (London: SPCK, 2007), p. 11.

8 See James Farwell, 'Baptism, Eucharist, and the Hospitality of Jesus: On the Practice of "Open Communion"', *Anglican Theological Review* 86:2 (2004), pp. 215–38, and the rejoinder Kathryn Tanner, 'In Praise of Open Communion: A Rejoinder to James Farwell', *Anglican Theological Review* 86:3 (2004), pp. 473–85.

9 Farwell, 'Baptism', p. 235.

10 John Milbank, 'Stale Expressions: The Management-Shaped Church', *Studies in Christian Ethics* 21:1 (2008), pp. 119–20.

11 Robin Gill and Derek Burke, *Strategic Church Leadership* (London: SPCK, 1996), p. 54.

12 Gill and Burke, *Strategic Church Leadership*, pp. 1–2.

13 Gill and Burke, *Strategic Church Leadership*, p. 70.

14 Gill and Burke, *Strategic Church Leadership*, p. 86.

15 Robin Gill and Derek Burke, 'Strategic Church Leadership' in John Adair and John Nelson (eds), *Creative Church Leadership* (Norwich: Canterbury Press, 2004), p. 66.

16 Gill and Burke, 'Strategic Church Leadership', p. 66.

17 Richard H. Roberts, 'Order and Organization: The Future of Institutional and Established Religion' in G. R. Evans and Martyn Percy (eds), *Managing the Church: Order and Organization in a Secular Age* (Sheffield: Sheffield Academic Press, 2000), p. 79.

18 Roberts, 'Order and Organization', pp. 80, 87.

19 Richard H. Roberts, *Religion, Theology and the Human Sciences* (Cambridge: Cambridge University Press, 2002), p. 163.

20 Malcolm Torry, *Managing God's Business* (Aldershot: Ashgate, 2005), p. 142.

21 Torry, *Managing God's Business*, pp. 140–3.

22 Gill and Burke, 'Strategic Church Leadership', p. 73.

23 Kenneth Leech, *Spirituality and Pastoral Care* (London: Sheldon Press, 1987), p. 8.

24 <www.kanuga.org/conference-calendar/conference-calendar-details/enneagram-conference>.

6 The household of God

1 Roger Scruton, *Green Philosophy: How to Think Seriously about the Planet* (London: Atlantic Books, 2012).

2 Anonymous, 'Letter to Diognetus' in *Early Christian Writings*, tr. Maxwell Staniforth (London: Penguin, 1968), p. 5.

3 Theano S. Terkenli, 'Home as a Region', *Geographical Review* 86:3 (July 1995), pp. 325–6.

4 Terkenli, 'Home as Region', p. 325.

5 Terkenli, 'Home as Region', p. 326.

6 Alison Blunt and Ann Varley, 'Geographies of Home', *Cultural Geographies* 11:3 (2004), p. 3.

7 Eamon Duffy, *The Voices of Morebath: Reformation and Rebellion in an English Village* (New Haven, CT: Yale University Press, 2001).

8 Wayne A. Meeks, *The First Urban Christians: The Social World of the Apostle Paul* (New Haven, CT: Yale University Press, 1983), p. 75.

9 Meeks, *The First Urban Christians*, p. 75.

10 Meeks, *The First Urban Christians*, p. 76.

11 Meeks, *The First Urban Christians*, pp. 76–7.

12 For example, Galatians 6.10; Ephesians 2.19; 1 Timothy 3.5, 15.

13 Ephesians 2.12–20.

14 Ephesians 2.21–22.

15 1 Timothy 3.15.

16 For this and subsequent quotes, see Geoffrey Chaucer, *The Canterbury Tales: Nine Tales and the General Prologue*, 'Prologue', ll. 477–528, ed. V. A. Kolve (New York: W. W. Norton, 1989), pp. 15–16.

17 *John Myrc: Instructions for Parish Priests*, ed. Edward Peacock (London: Early English Text Society, 1868), ll. 51–2.

18 Peacock, *John Myrc: Instructions*, ll. 69–80, 87–120, 143–207.

19 Peacock, *John Myrc: Instructions*, ll. 1951–2024.

20 George Herbert, *The Country Parson, The Temple*, ed. by John N. Wall (New York: Paulist Press, 1981), p. 75.

21 Herbert, *The Country Parson*, p. 71.

22 Herbert, *The Country Parson*, p. 87.

23 Herbert, *The Country Parson*, p. 78.

24 Scruton, *Green Philosophy*, p. 3.

25 Scruton, *Green Philosophy*, p. 27.
26 Scruton, *Green Philosophy*, pp. 209–10.
27 Scruton, *Green Philosophy*, pp. 210–11.
28 Scruton, *Green Philosophy*, p. 211.
29 Scruton, *Green Philosophy*, p. 214.
30 Scruton, *Green Philosophy*, p. 214.
31 Scruton, *Green Philosophy*, p. 216.
32 Scruton, *Green Philosophy*, p. 216.
33 Scruton, *Green Philosophy*, p. 227.
34 Scruton, *Green Philosophy*, p. 228.
35 Scruton, *Green Philosophy*, p. 229.
36 Scruton, *Green Philosophy*, p. 231.
37 Scruton, *Green Philosophy*, p. 253.
38 See, for example, Augustine, *Homilies on the Gospel of John* (1–40), 3.21, tr. Edmund Hill OP (Hyde Park, NY: New City Press, 2009).
39 Augustine, *On Christian Teaching*, 1.8, tr. R. P. H. Green (Oxford: Oxford University Press, 1997).
40 Augustine, *On Christian Teaching*, 1.7–8.

7 Principles for a domestic Church

1 Rowan Williams, *Why Study the Past? The Quest for the Historical Church* (London: Darton, Longman & Todd, 2005), p. 35.
2 For further reading, see Tom Wright, *The Challenge of Jesus* (London: SPCK, 2000).
3 Williams, *Why Study the Past?*, p. 54.
4 Williams, *Why Study the Past?*, p. 55.
5 William T. Cavanaugh, *Being Consumed: Economics and Christian Desire* (Grand Rapids, MI: Eerdmans, 2008), pp. 54–5.
6 Kenneth Leech, *Spirituality and Pastoral Care* (London: Sheldon Press, 1987), p. 127.
7 Leech, *Spirituality and Pastoral Care*, p. 130.
8 Michael Ramsey, *The Christian Priest Today* (London: SPCK, 1972).
9 1 Corinthians 12.26.
10 1 Corinthians 10.1–12.
11 Rowan Williams, *Faith in the Public Square* (London: Bloomsbury Continuum, 2012), p. 1.
12 Genesis 28.15.
13 Genesis 28.17.

References

Books and articles

Adair, John and Nelson, John (eds), *Creative Church Leadership* (Norwich: Canterbury Press, 2004).

Anderson, Walter Truett, *The Upstart Spring: Esalen and the Human Potential Movement: The First Twenty Years* (Boston, MA: Addison-Wesley, 1983).

Anonymous, 'Letter to Diognetus' in *Early Christian Writings*, tr. Maxwell Staniforth (London: Penguin, 1968).

Arsenault, Amelia H. and Castells, Manuel, 'The Structure and Dynamics of Global Multi-Media Business Networks' *International Journal of Communication* 2 (2008), pp. 707–48.

Augustine, *Essential Sermons*, tr. Edmund Hill OP (Hyde Park, NY: New City Press, 2007).

——, *Homilies on the Gospel of John* (1–40), tr. Edmund Hill OP (Hyde Park, NY: New City Press, 2009).

——, *On Christian Teaching*, tr. R. P. H. Green (Oxford: Oxford University Press, 1997).

Bauman, Zygmunt, *Consuming Life* (Cambridge: Polity Press, 2011).

Beales III, J. Howard, 'Advertising to Kids and the FTC: A Regulatory Retrospective that Advises the Present', *George Mason Law Review* 12:4 (April 2004), pp. 873–94.

Bernays, Edward L., 'Engineering Consent', *Annals of the American Academy of Political and Social Science* 250 (March 1947), pp. 113–20.

——, 'Moulding Public Opinion', *Annals of the American Academy of Political and Social Science* 179 (May 1935), pp. 82–7.

Blunt, Alison and Dowling, Robyn, *Home* (Abingdon: Routledge, 2006).

Blunt, Alison and Varley, Ann, 'Geographies of Home', *Cultural Geographies* 11:3 (2004), pp. 3–6.

Boorstin, Daniel, *The Image: A Guide to Pseudo-Events in America* (New York: Vintage Books, 1992).

Brown, Brené, *The Gifts of Imperfection: Let Go of Who You Think You're Supposed to Be and Embrace Who You Are* (Center City, MN: Hazelden, 2010).

Brown, Callum, *The Death of Christian Britain* (London: Routledge, 2009).

Budde, Michael L., 'The Rational Shepherd: Corporate Practices and the Church', *Studies in Christian Ethics* 21:1 (2008), pp. 96–116.

References

Campbell, Heidi and La Pastina, Antonio C., 'How the iPhone Became Divine: New Media, Religion and the Intertextual Circulation of Meaning' *New Media & Society* 12:7 (2010), pp. 1197–207.

Carlson, Les and Grossbart, Sanford, 'Parental Style and Consumer Socialization', *Journal of Consumer Research* 15:1 (June 1988), pp. 77–94.

Castell, Manuel, *The Rise of the Network Society*, 2nd edn (Chichester: John Wiley & Sons Ltd, 2007).

Cavanaugh, William T., *Being Consumed: Economics and Christian Desire* (Grand Rapids, MI: Eerdmans, 2008).

Chaney, David, 'Subtopia in Gateshead: The MetroCentre as a Cultural Form', *Theory, Culture & Society* 7 (1990), pp. 49–68.

Chaucer, Geoffrey, *The Canterbury Tales: Nine Tales and the General Prologue*, ed. V. A. Kolve (New York: W. W. Norton, 1989).

Christakis, Dimitri A., Zimmerman, Frederick J., DiGiuseppe, David L. and McCarty, Carolyn A., 'Early Television Exposure and Subsequent Attentional Problems in Children', *Pediatrics* 113 (2004), pp. 708–13.

Cova, Bernard, Kozinets, Robert and Shankar, Avi, *Consumer Tribes* (Oxford: Butterworth-Heinemann, 2007).

Cross, Gary, *Men to Boys: The Making of Modern Immaturity* (New York: Cambridge University Press, 2008).

Davie, Grace, 'From Obligation to Consumption: A Framework for Reflection on Northern Europe', *Political Theology* 6:3 (2005), pp. 281–301.

——, *Religion in Britain since 1945* (Oxford: Blackwell, 1994).

Davison, Andrew and Milbank, Alison, *For the Parish: A Critique of Fresh Expressions* (London: SCM Press, 2010).

Dijk, Jan van, *The Information Age: Social Aspects of New Media*, 3rd edn (London: Sage, 2012).

Du Plessis, Erik, *The Branded Mind: What Neuroscience Really Tells Us about the Puzzle of the Brain and the Brand* (London: Kogan Page, 2011).

Duffy, Eamon, *The Voices of Morebath: Reformation and Rebellion in an English Village* (New Haven, CT: Yale University Press, 2001).

Evans, G. R., 'The Ecclesiology of the Turnbull Report' in G. R. Evans and Martyn Percy, *Managing the Church: Order and Organization in a Secular Age* (Sheffield: Sheffield Academic Press, 2000), pp. 97–107.

Evans, G. R. and Percy, Martyn, *Managing the Church: Order and Organization in a Secular Age* (Sheffield: Sheffield Academic Press, 2000).

Farwell, James, 'Baptism, Eucharist, and the Hospitality of Jesus: On the Practice of "Open Communion"', *Anglican Theological Review* 86:2 (2004), pp. 215–38.

France, Alan, Meredith, Joanne and Murdoch, Graham, 'Children and Marketing Literature: Final Report, CRSP 583' (Loughborough: CRSP, 2008).

Giddens, Anthony, *Consequences of Modernity* (Palo Alto, CA: Stanford University Press, 1990).

——, *Modernity and Self-Identity: Self and Society in the Late Modern Age* (Palo Alto, CA: Stanford University Press, 2001).

Gill, Robin and Burke, Derek, *Strategic Church Leadership* (London: SPCK, 1996).

——, 'Strategic Church Leadership' in John Adair and John Nelson (eds), *Creative Church Leadership* (Norwich: Canterbury Press, 2004), pp. 62–74.

Goldman, Marion, *The American Soul Rush: Esalen and the Rise of Spiritual Privilege* (New York: New York University Press, 2012).

Goodhew, David, Roberts, Andrew and Volland, Michael, *Fresh! An Introduction to Fresh Expressions of Church and Pioneer Ministry* (London: SCM Press, 2012).

Halpern, Jack, *Fame Junkies: The Hidden Truth Behind America's Favorite Addiction* (Boston, MA: Houghton Mifflin, 2007).

Hauerwas, Stanley, *A Community of Character* (South Bend, IN: University of Notre Dame Press, 1981).

Herbert, George, *The Country Parson, The Temple*, ed. John N. Wall (New York: Paulist Press, 1981).

Hymowitz, Kay, *Manning Up: How the Rise of Women has Turned Men into Boys* (New York: Basic Books, 2011).

Kiley, Dan, *Peter Pan Syndrome: Men Who Have Never Grown Up* (New York: Avon Books, 1983).

Lanier, Jaron, *You Are Not a Gadget* (London: Penguin, 2010).

Larson, Erik, *The Naked Consumer: How our Private Lives Became Public Commodities* (New York: Henry Holt & Co., 1992).

Lasch, Christopher, *The Culture of Narcissism: American Life in an Age of Diminishing Expectations* (New York: W. W. Norton & Co., 1981).

Leech, Kenneth, *Spirituality and Pastoral Care* (London: Sheldon Press, 1987).

McAlister, Anna R. and Cornwell, T. Bettina, 'Children's Brand Symbolism Understanding: Links to Theory of Mind and Executive Functioning', *Psychology and Marketing* 27:3 (March 2010), pp. 203–28.

McCracken, Grant David, *Culture and Consumption* (Bloomington, IN: Indiana University Press, 1990).

McIntyre, Alasdair, *After Virtue* (South Bend, IN: University of Notre Dame Press, 2007).

Maffesoli, Michael, *The Time of the Tribes: The Decline of Individualism in Mass Society* (London: Sage, 1995).

Mead, Rebecca, *One Perfect Day: The Selling of the American Wedding* (New York: Penguin, 2008).

Meeks, Wayne A., *The First Urban Christians: The Social World of the Apostle Paul* (New Haven, CT: Yale University Press, 1983).

References

Milbank, John, 'Stale Expressions: The Management-Shaped Church', *Studies in Christian Ethics* 21:1 (2008), pp. 119–20.

Miles, Steven, *Consumerism – as a Way of Life* (London: Sage, 1998).

Miller, Vincent, *Consuming Religion: Christian Faith and Practice in a Consumer Culture* (London: Continuum, 2005).

Moore, R. Laurence, *Selling God: American Religion in the Marketplace of Culture* (Oxford: Oxford University Press, 2004).

Myrc, John, *Instructions for Parish Priests*, ed. Edward Peacock (London: Early English Text Society, 1868).

Nelstrop, Louise and Percy, Martyn (eds), *Evaluating Fresh Expressions* (Norwich: Canterbury Press, 2008).

O'Donovan, Oliver, *Common Objects of Love: Moral Reflection and the Shaping of Community* (Grand Rapids, MI: Eerdmans, 2002).

——, *The Desire of the Nations: Rediscovering the Roots of Political Theology* (Cambridge: Cambridge University Press, 1996).

O'Donovan, Oliver and O'Donovan, Joan Lockwood (eds), *From Irenaeus to Grotius: A Sourcebook in Christian Political Thought* (Grand Rapids, MI: Eerdmans, 1999).

Percy, Martyn, *Engaging with Contemporary Culture: Christianity, Theology, and the Concrete Church* (Aldershot: Ashgate, 2005).

——, 'Old Tricks for New Dogs? A Critique of Fresh Expressions' in L. Nelstrop and M. Percy (eds), *Evaluating Fresh Expressions* (Norwich: Canterbury Press, 2008), pp. 27–39.

Poole, Eve, 'Baptizing Management', *Studies in Christian Ethics* 21:1 (2008), pp. 83–95.

Ramsey, Michael, *The Gospel and the Catholic Church* (London: Longmans, 1956).

Renvoisé, Patrick and Morin, Christophe, *Neuromarketing: Understanding the 'Buy Buttons' in Your Customer's Brain* (Nashville, TN: Thomas Nelson, 2010).

Rieff, Philip, *The Triumph of the Therapeutic: Uses of Faith after Freud* (Wilmington, DE: ISI Books, 2006).

Ritzer, George, *The McDonaldization of Society* (London: Sage, 2004).

Robbin, Mike, *Be Yourself, Everyone Else is Already Taken: Transform Your Life with the Power of Authenticity* (San Francisco, CA: Jossey-Bass, 2009).

Roberts, Richard H., 'Order and Organization: The Future of Institutional and Established Religion' in G. R. Evans and Martyn Percy (eds), *Managing the Church: Order and Organization in a Secular Age* (Sheffield: Sheffield Academic Press, 2000), pp. 78–95.

——, 'Personhood and Performance: Managerialism, Post-Democracy and the Ethics of "Enrichment"', *Studies in Christian Ethics* 21:61 (2008), pp. 61–82.

——, *Religion, Theology and the Human Sciences* (Cambridge: Cambridge University Press, 2002).

Rojek, Chris, *Celebrity* (London: Reaktion Books Ltd, 2001).

Rosack, Jim, 'Brain Scans Reveal Physiology of ADHD', *Psychiatric News* 39:1 (2004), pp. 26–7.

Rosen, Christine, *Preaching Eugenics: Religious Leaders and the American Eugenics Movement* (New York: Oxford University Press, 2004).

Ryan, John, Wentworth, William and Chapman, Gabrielle, 'Models of Emotions in Therapeutic Self-Help Books', *Sociological Spectrum* 14 (1994), pp. 241–55.

Scruton, Roger, *Green Philosophy: How to Think Seriously about the Planet* (London: Atlantic Books, 2012).

Tanner, Kathryn, 'In Praise of Open Communion: A Rejoinder to James Farwell', *Anglican Theological Review* 86:3 (2004), pp. 473–85.

Terkenli, Theano S., 'Home as a Region', *Geographical Review* 86:3 (July 1995), pp. 324–34.

Torry, Malcolm, *Managing God's Business* (Aldershot: Ashgate, 2005).

Towner, Philip, *The Letters to Timothy and Titus* (Grand Rapids, MI: Eerdmans, 2006).

Turner, Graeme, *Understanding Celebrity* (London: Sage, 2004).

Ulrich, David, *Human Resource Champions: The Next Agenda for Adding Value and Delivering Results* (Boston, MA: Harvard Business School, 1996).

Williams, Rowan, *Faith in the Public Square* (London: Bloomsbury Continuum, 2012).

——, *Why Study the Past? The Quest for the Historical Church* (London: Darton, Longman & Todd, 2005).

Wright, Tom, *The Challenge of Jesus* (London: SPCK, 2000).

Yaconelli, Mark, *Growing Souls: Experiments in Contemplative Youth Ministry* (London: SPCK, 2007).

Reports

'British Social Attitudes' survey (London: National Centre for Social Research, 2012).

Buckingham, D., 'The Impact of the Commercial World on Children's Wellbeing: Report of an Independent Assessment' (London: DCSF/DCM, 2009), 5.5.

Margo, Julia, Dixon, Mike, Pearce, Nick and Reed, Howard, *Freedom's Orphans: Raising Youth in a Changing World* (London: Institute for Public Policy Research, 2006).

Mission-shaped Church: Church Planting and Fresh Expressions of Church in a Changing Context (London: Church House Publishing, 2004).

Public Law 96–252, 94 Stat. 374 (28 May 1980): 'Federal Trade Commission Improvements Act of 1980'.

Working as One Body: The Report of the Archbishops' Commission on the Organisation of the Church of England (London: Church House Publishing, 1995).

Websites and media

BBC, *The Century of the Self*, directed and produced by Adam Curtis, first broadcast in 2002.

ESA, 'Essential Facts of the Computer and Video Game Industry' (2011), <www.theesa.com/facts/pdfs/ESA_EF_2011.pdf> (accessed 5 March 2012).

Herdman, Sophie, 'Online Pornography: House of Commons Debate', *Psychologies*, 25 November 2010, <www.psychologies.co.uk/culture/house-of-commons-debate-online-pornography.html> (accessed 23 April 2012).

Johnson, Branwell, 'Habbo research shows teens no longer join one tribe', *Marketing Weekly*, 10 January <www.marketingweek.co.uk/habbo-research-shows-teens-no-longer-join-one-tribe/3004729.article> (accessed 23 February 2012).

Johnson, Po and Merryman, Ashley, 'The Creativity Crisis', *Newsweek*, 10 July 2010, <www.thedailybeast.com/newsweek/2010/07/10/the-creativity-crisis.html> (accessed 6 April 2012).

Hutcheon, Linda, 'Irony, Nostalgia, and the Postmodern', University of Toronto English Library (1998), <www.library.utoronto.ca/utel/criticism/hutchinp.html> (accessed 25 May 2012).

'Marketing to Children: Trillion Dollar Kids', *The Economist*, 30 November 2006, <www.economist.com/node/8355035> (accessed 26 February 2012).

PBS (Public Broadcasting Service in the USA), 'Merchants of Cool', *Frontline*, 1 February 2001.

Reich, Robert, 'The Decline of the Public Good', 4 January 2012, <www.robertreich.org/post/15331903866> (accessed 10 February 2012).

Printed and bound by CPI Group (UK) Ltd, Croydon, CR0 4YY

13/04/2025

14656473-0004